To Wisconsin State University Library

Stevens Point

Compliments of :

Wisconsin State Grange

Edwin Sommers, Master - 1966

First Century of
Service and Evolution

THE GRANGE
1867-1967

by
W. L. ROBINSON

The National Grange
1616 H Street, N. W.
Washington, D. C.

ABOUT THE AUTHOR

by Raymond W. Miller

WILLIAM L. ROBINSON is a prolific editor and writer, with knowledge and experience in the fields of farm business, cooperation, business history, and traffic safety. He is a former newspaperman and magazine editor and is a member of the National Press Club. He has directed the production of many educational films and was, for the past three years, chairman of the National Committee on Films for Safety.

For almost two decades he has edited *American Cooperation,* the annual yearbook on farm business published by the American Institute of Cooperation.

As Editor of *Sportsmanlike Driving* and *Teaching Driver and Traffic Safety Education,* as well as supplementary driver education teaching aids for the American Automobile Association, he has produced materials that are the standard in U.S. high schools, with millions of young drivers thus learning rules of the road and proper attitude toward other highway users. His work in this field has gained for him national and international reputation.

As a professional "book architect" he has worked with a dozen authors in the production of a wide variety of books ranging from biography, capitalism vs. communism, and agricultural cooperation, in addition to those subjects mentioned above.

Mr. Robinson is a successful farmer of Travilah, Md., producing eggs and cattle.

With this rich background, the National Grange sought his services to produce this concise 100-year history for its Centennial Year. The National Grange believes he has conceived and written an outstanding volume which deserves to receive widespread attention and acceptance in the Centennial Year and into the future.

Foreword

NORMAN ROCKWELL, a long-time Grange member, Seventh Degree Patron of Husbandry—Joined with the Vermont State Grange, in presenting his charcoal portrait of the National Master at the National Grange Session in Burlington, Vt., in 1953.

A Century of Service and Evolution

THE GRANGE
1867-1967

This has been a very significant century of America's history.

Important contributions to the development of proper, constructive relationships between government and its people have been evolved or substantially influenced by the Order of Patrons of Husbandry. Now, as the Grange is about to enter its second *Century of Service and Evolution* —and of inspiration and motivation of its own people—we must be increasingly cognizant of the relationships between government and important segments of society, as well as the relationship of economic groups within that society.

The Grange was conceived and brought into being to stimulate the rural people, both farm and non-farm, and to dignify as well as lighten their labor by diffusing knowledge and expanding the human mind. It has thus raised the horizons and improved the opportunities of individuals, but has recognized at the same time that human happiness depends upon general prosperity. The very program and history of the Grange is as broad as all rural life itself.

Indeed, the history of the world is but the history of organization; and demonstrates alike its necessity and its beneficence. The philosophy of self-government, as we know it in America, therefore places greater importance on proper and effective organizational structure within our whole American society than does any other philosophy of organized society.

An organization is *not* like a chain—no stronger than its weakest link. On the contrary, an organization gains strength in proportion to the combined strength and effectiveness of its members. Hence each of us has a direct and personal interest—as well as a civic, moral, and political responsibility—to exert reasonable effort and to assist in perfecting appropriate organization to stimulate and combine the highest purposes and more constructive efforts of men, women, and families of each of our communities. Thus we tend to insure that future service and evolution shall be of the highest and most worthy character.

Grange Achievements a Commanding Challenge

The record of the Grange stands as a solid platform from which we may proceed. The achievements of our organization are, within themselves, a commanding challenge. We are far better prepared to accept the responsibilities of a great self-governing society by reason of our organizational experience and seniority. In such acceptance, we shall, in large measure, be able to enjoy richer and fuller family and community life. As our society becomes increasingly plenteous and bountiful—rich and rewarding in experiences and associations—the Grange must then stimulate us to achieve the following goals:

1. A higher and better manhood and womanhood among ourselves.

2. Being never afraid of grace and beauty, which will protect and enhance our environment, our homes, and our communities.

3. Increasing our individual wisdom, that we may in reasonable measure match the fabulous growth in the world's total knowledge, characterizing our days with a reasonably comparable growth in ourselves.

4. Raising the standards of our own moral, cultural, and social achievements, that we may deserve, and in due course, command the respect of our neighbors.

As author of this concise, 128-page, readable and meaningful statement of the philosophy, purpose, and significance that has underlaid the first century of the Grange, W. L. (Bill) Robinson has given evidences of the wisdom and skill with which the Order of Patrons of Husbandry was conceived and brought into being. He has briefly outlined the kind of contribution that its organizational structure has made to its members; and which the members have thereby found to be such a useful institution in influencing the course of their own lives, their own communities and, indeed, of the very society of which you and I are now a part.

The Founders of the Order of Patrons of Husbandry were not isolation-ists. They laid the framework for the world's only farm and rural family fraternity. They handed us an organization capable of stimulating the in-dividual in the community interest, and also well structured to build a better community in the interest of families and individual members thereof.

A careful study of this brief synopsis of the Grange and its history will leave no doubt that these same goals and organizational purposes, that have served America so well for 100 years, provide a solid and challenging foundation for building a second century of service as we look forward to an America which will give increased attention to *equity* and *justice*, out of which can come boundless progress for a great nation and its people.

Needed—The Best Grange We Can Build

You and I, and the community in which we may live, therefore, need the best Grange that we can build. Whether our interest in agriculture is direct or indirect, we have that interest. We should each, therefore, also be interested in this great agricultural institution and organization of the Grange, dedicated to the fundamental principle that the rural home must be a bright and happy place in which to live and to rear a family.

The Founders of the Grange were bold. They championed property rights and human rights. But they accepted responsibility and insisted that their fellow Americans do likewise. So must we.

They sought to build an organization which would inspire and incite a degree of self-discipline, even as they recognized the necessity of organ-ized discipline in achieving an orderly society.

Clearly, the increasingly complex inter-relationships and mutual inter-dependence of producer and consumer; that of the rural non-farm family and the strictly agricultural family within the community; and the inter-relationships and inter-*dependence* of one community, one state, or even one nation with another, all these factors *in our decade* of the 1960's in-crease and underline the importance of the basic philosophy and purpose that inspired the Founders of the Order of Patrons of Husbandry.

Is it not clear, therefore, that we need something much more substantial than a mere ordinary kind of an organization? Let us, therefore, plan wisely to build the Grange; even as we have had to better equip ourselves in our respective enterprises. Let us increase the usefulness and improve the effectiveness of the Order of Patrons of Husbandry, that it may serve us better, even as we ourselves serve society in general—through the Grange.

HERSCHEL D. NEWSOM
National Master,
The National Grange

Officers of the National Grange

William J. Brake
Lecturer

A. Lars Nelson
Overseer

John W. Scott
Secretary

Mrs. Ethel Davis
Ceres

Mrs. Bernice Knight
Pomona

Mrs. Betty K. Hall
Flora

Mrs. Doris R. Kershner
Lady Asst. Steward

Harry D. Ritchey
Steward

Herschel D. Newsom
Master

Allen P. Wheeler
Chaplain

LOREN MURPHY
Assistant Steward

LIONEL BURGESS
Treasurer

WOODROW W. TUCKER
Gatekeeper

Harry B. Caldwell
Executive Committee

Maynard C. Dolloff
Executive Committee

James W. Ingwersen
Executive Committee

Ermil S. Jerome
Executive Committee

Contents

ORGANIZATIONAL CHART OF NATIONAL GRANGE

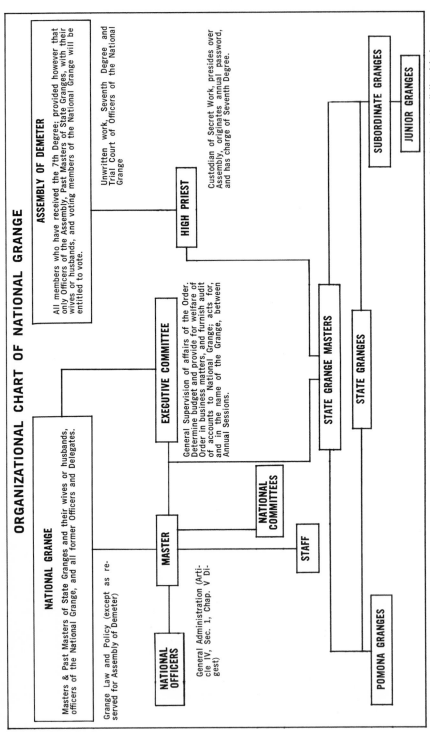

ASSEMBLY OF DEMETER

All members who have received the 7th Degree; provided however that only Officers of the Assembly, Past Masters of State Granges, with their wives or husbands, and voting members of the National Grange will be entitled to vote.

Unwritten work, Seventh Degree and Trial Court of Officers of the National Grange

HIGH PRIEST

Custodian of Secret Work, presides over Assembly, originates annual password, and has charge of Seventh Degree.

NATIONAL GRANGE

Masters & Past Masters of State Granges and their wives or husbands, the officers of the National Grange, and all former Officers and Delegates.

Grange Law and Policy (except as reserved for Assembly of Demeter)

EXECUTIVE COMMITTEE

General Supervision of affairs of the Order. Determine budget and provide for welfare of Order in business matters, and furnish audit of accounts to National Grange; acts for, and in the name of the Grange, between Annual Sessions.

MASTER

General Administration (Article IV, Sec. 1, Chap. V Digest)

NATIONAL COMMITTEES

STAFF

NATIONAL OFFICERS

STATE GRANGE MASTERS

STATE GRANGES

POMONA GRANGES

SUBORDINATE GRANGES

JUNIOR GRANGES

The National Grange Charters and provides Dispensation to State, Pomona, Subordinate, and Junior Granges; each exercises Organizational (as distinguished from Policy) Jurisdiction over each through State Masters who are also Delegates (with wives or husbands) in the National Grange.

Introduction
Dream of the Founders

This 100-year history of the Grange could never have been written had it not been for the glowing achievements of a few inspired, dynamic pioneers, followed by the steady, continuing efforts of millions of hardy, high-principled, sensible men and women who built magnificently over the years.

The founder, OLIVER HUDSON KELLEY, and six other far-sighted men of different abilities—but vital for this great purpose—dreamed the dream of a helpful, protective, energetic organization with lofty ideals of fraternity and brotherhood, along with down-to-earth services to neighbors, community, state, and nation.

Many thousand words have been written about living and farming conditions in the 1860's and the personal attributes of "Father" Kelley. Grange history books are filled with stories about the early hopes and aspirations that brought these seven founders together.

Each contributed in a purposeful way toward developing the whole.

Among all the historical writings about the happenings that led to the founding of the Grange none seems more intriguing to this observer than the Address by Mrs. Eva McDowell, widow of one of the Founders, Francis M. McDowell, 50 years ago at the Golden Jubilee Celebration of the Grange in Washington, D.C., November 18, 1916.

Mrs. McDowell knew them all and heard much about the early days from the lips of her husband. She regretted that she did not question them more, personally, when she had the opportunity. It seemed to her, she said, that they would live forever!

OFFICE OF WILLIAM SAUNDERS, one of the Founders and the first National Master. He was the Superintendent of the Propagating Gardens of the U. S. Department of Agriculture. In his office, this small brick building at Missouri Avenue and 4½ Street, Washington, D. C., the Founders held their first meetings and developed the Grange. The names of the Seven Founders are inscribed on the Birthplace Marker, dedicated September 9, 1951, and placed near the site of this building.

WM. SAUNDERS

F. M. McDOWELL

JOHN TRIMBLE

O. H. KELLEY

A. B. GROSH

J. R. THOMPSON

W. M. IRELAND

FOUNDERS OF THE PATRONS OF HUSBANDRY.

What impressed her most about these seven men were the so-apparently different characteristics they possessed and which they brought to full force in their development of the Grange idea.

Proof of their varying abilities is the organization that has stood the test for 100 years, and now goes into its second century with essentially the same lofty ideals, ritual, and practical mechanics of procedure—but improved, of course, by 20th Century modes of operation, better communication, more resources.

It was said that in the beginning "Father" Kelley sat down by himself and tried to formulate a ritual and a constitution for a farmer's organization but found it a hopeless task—having no special ability along that line. He had a great dream, though, and coupled it with initiative and rare foresight by applying to others for help so that in the end there came about the magic number of seven, the perfect number.

OLIVER KELLEY excelled as a propagandist and was chosen by the others to go out into the world (as did Paul) and preach the Grange gospel. He was eminently fitted for this work.

To WILLIAM SAUNDERS belongs credit for the plan of organization. He advocated establishing township, county, state, and national bodies. The title "Subordinate" was substituted for the word "township" and later when the county Grange seemed impractical, the term "Pomona" was established for it. Mr. Saunders suggested the name "Grange" for the meeting place, and the title of "Patrons of Husbandry" for the Order.

JOHN R. THOMPSON was a high degree Mason and had given much thought to ritual and laws of fraternity. He was largely responsible for the ritual of the Grange, having written that of the Sixth and Seventh Degrees, and corrected and approved that of the lower degrees.

WILLIAM M. IRELAND was also a Mason of high degree. He was expert in parliamentary law and journalism, and to him belongs the framework of the constitution and bylaws, and the preparation of the journals of proceedings of the early sessions for the printer.

AARON B. GROSH was also skilled in ritualism, but his chief work for the Order was that of furnishing all the prayers for the lower degrees, which he helped to write. To him, Grangers are indebted for the high moral tone without religious bias which comes all through the Ritual. He also recognized the value of song in the Grange meetings, and gathered the first group of Grange melodies.

JOHN TRIMBLE acted as critic and adviser. So often did he pounce upon a pet idea of some of the others, pick it all to pieces and point out all its flaws, that he became known as "the wet blanket of the Order." Second thought nearly always demonstrated the justice of his criticisms, and they were generally heeded. On the other hand, he was just as ready to praise when he considered the work good, and his associates learned to await with eagerness his characteristic "well done," and drew deep breaths of relief when they heard it.

FRANCIS M. MCDOWELL, the last to become associated with the other six, found them with no definite financial plan, each one paying out of his own pocket such sums as he could spare for the work from time to time, keeping no accounts, having no idea of what they should do with their funds if they ever became strong enough to accumulate any. They gladly turned their affairs over to him and he took charge and remained in charge for the remainder of his life. It was through him that a happy investment in government bonds was made with the first surplus funds, which gave them sufficient income to tide them over the years of depression, and enabled them to follow through without incurring debt. Mr. McDowell served as treasurer for nearly 21 years from January, 1873, to November, 1893.

In Mrs. McDowell's words:

"To sum up, we have here a propagandist, an organizer, a ritualist, a parliamentarian and journalist, a man of God, a critic, and a financier. Could any one of these have given us our Order as we have it today? Could more than these have made it any better?"

HOME OF OLIVER HUDSON KELLEY, at the Kelley Farm near Elk River, Minnesota. This is now a National Historic Landmark, the Kelley Farm now being the property of the Minnesota Historical Society.

I

The Grange Today

The nation's leading self-help community group, where one meets neighbors—both town and country—makes new friends, and learns to know old ones better. He works with them to build a better place in which to live and raise a family.

The Grange is a voice for rural people, a legislative representative, an opportunity to develop personal abilities, a force which emphasizes family, home and agriculture, and concern for others based on our religious heritage.

GRANGE YOUTH RECEIVE ON-THE-SPOT EDUCATION—*A group of Ohio Grange youth and their parents stand on the steps of the Capitol during a recent visit to Washington. Many school officials encourage youth participation in Grange-sponsored short tours during the school term. Each visit stresses how the government works and the importance of the individual citizen. Such trips include a visit to National Grange headquarters.*

Importance, Excitement, Satisfaction of Grange Membership

Being a Grange member sets that man, that woman, that boy, that girl apart!

The Grange is a vital, tremendous organization with many satisfying elements. The Grange member not only becomes interested but actively engaged as he realizes the double objectives of participation:

1. Benefiting through the many personal and family advantages of membership.
2. Serving his neighbors, community, state, and nation by personal and group activities—worthwhile and important.

Not only do the benefits of membership make life more complete and pleasurable for members, but Grange service and legislative accomplishments help millions of people outside the membership.

Family Unity a Major Grange Objective

Unique in its family and fraternal structure among organizations anywhere in the world, the Grange is based on the solid foundation of the American farm and rural family from which it derives its strength, its progressive character, and its tolerance born out of a high moral tone without religious bias.

Members are largely property-owning people of a dependable and stable citizenship. They are eager to not only enjoy, and continue to enjoy, the benefits of that citizenship but want to take their places in an active America as knowledgeable, worthy citizens. They seek a satisfying and satisfactory family life, with growing, upright children who also become stable, top-grade citizens. They want to feel that their abilities

7

are being used, and their influence *means something* not only in their local Grange but in the development of policies for state, national, and world-wide accomplishments of substantial worth.

As a community family fraternity, the Grange combines its practical features with a beautiful ritual which depicts the finest features and traditions of the American family and country life. The Grange cooperates with the church, the school and every other American institution whose aims for progress and the enrichment of life are similar.

It has been said that no other secular association in America, of people who voluntarily group themselves together, has within it so much of religion with so little sectarianism; no other with so much patriotism with so little partisanship. The American flag must be on display at every Grange meeting. The open Bible is on the altar in full view of all members.

The Grange is one of the very few places where the whole family—all ages—may attend together for sociability, education, and to meet other families on a common level of understanding.

The Grange provides regular meetings for business and discussion as well as literary programs for sociability and education. An active member acquires many fine fraternal friends.

EVERYBODY TAKES PART—Rehearsing for some entertainment at a State Grange Youth Leadership camp are members of the South Dakota Grange. Although there are active programs for men and women in the different age groups, the Grange emphasizes family participation in most work and play projects.

Grange Accomplishments Helped Preserve America

While the Grange is non-partisan, it does take part in community life. It does not support any particular candidate for public office but maintains a lively interest and activity in local, state, and national legislation. Its accomplishments in this field throughout the first century of its life have been astounding with far-reaching effects. The record shows that, without doubt, the Grange has helped to preserve the American way of life we enjoy today.

The far-sighted pioneers who started the Grange 100 years ago were truly remarkable in their conception of the organization. Consider that it has served well the needs of farmers, rural and suburban communities, and the nation as a whole in all of these 100 years, and that *now in the "Jet" Age* it continues to fit right into the needs of rural and rur-urban people and can perform its mission today with little or no change in its procedures.

Now, some 6000 Subordinate Granges with a membership growing fast toward the one million mark continue to follow out the basic tenets of our nation. It can be rightly said that the Grange was authorized in the Bill of Rights when the First Amendment to the U. S. Constitution was created. This gave reference to "freedom of speech" and the right of people "peaceably to assemble."

At that early date in our history, the founders of our nation recognized that groups of people would need to unite, through meetings and discussions, through decisions and actions, in ways that they could perfect or reconcile positions among themselves, then present viewpoints and recommendations to the proper authorities, at the same time as they were learning to solve, through united action, local problems and needs.

The Grange is an exemplification of this idea in that it provides the organizational basis for people, and offers individual members who are united as to over-all purpose and philosophy the opportunity to influence the course of action in their communities, the county, the state, and the nation, or even in the world itself, through creating and supporting the policies of the National Grange.

In the Grange Hall dedication ceremony is this statement:

"Within the walls of this Grange home will be taught the noblest ideals of civilization. Here will be given the individual opportunity that trains men and women for larger usefulness and civic service; here new emphasis will be placed upon the home, its influence extended and its ties strengthened; here also will be taught loyalty to country and to God and the never-ceasing duty each human being owes to his fellows."

A Family Institution

"The woman's cause is man's: They rise or sink
Together."   —Tennyson

Unique because it brings together young and old, men and women, boys and girls, the Grange looks forward to its second 100 years as the greatest American family organization—cradle and developer of noble human aspirations; generator of closer, more satisfying relationships among man, wife and children, and their friends; fertilizer of ideas and generous actions to help neighbors and improve community life; site of exhilerating and sincere friendships and social activities.

"Your organization will never be permanent if you leave the women out!"

This is the forceful statement attributed to Miss Caroline Hall, "Father" Kelley's niece, whose vision and emphasis on what women could do for the Grange led her uncle and other Founders to decide, *for the first time in America,* that women should have equal status with men AND A VOTE.

While early records of discussions among the Founders contained no reference to women, the influence of his niece and then his own strong conviction led to Kelley's happy decision, and the inclusion of women in important basic ritual and other Grange activities.

One hundred years ago this was unusual and misunderstood—with some people still clinging to the old belief that any organization which admitted women to equality of membership *and privilege* was "going altogether too far."

Another of the Founders, Rev. A. B. Grosh, first Chaplain of the Grange, who had seconded Miss Hall's suggestion, and was faithful in translating her idea into the ritual, said in his book *"Mentor in the Granges,"* dedicated to his wife:

> Here is an Order inviting woman to an enlarged and cheerful social intercourse; to enlivening recreation for body and mind; to instructive lessons by pleasing symbols and scenic representations; to the improvement of mind, heart and morals by the programs of Grange meetings, and by conversations on a great variety of helpful subjects.

WITH FOOD COMES FELLOWSHIP—Conventioneers at the 1965 Grange Annual Session in Topeka line up for a buffalo barbecue. Buffets, smorgasbords, picnics and dinners are a feature of Granges across the nation.

Woman needs our Order far more than does the sterner, hardier sex; and the Order needs her for man's improvement. Her gentle influence, her innate tact in all matters of good taste and propriety, her instinctive perceptions of righteousness and purity—all these are needed in the Grange and also in society at large, from which she has been so much excluded, but into which our Order is rapidly introducing her.

Side by side with her husband should she advance in knowledge and wisdom, that she may be his helpmeet in all things. Onward and yet onward, before her advancing children, should she be enabled to progress in useful knowledge, that she may guide their tender feet in the ways of literature and science while she trains them to lives of virtue, usefulness and peace.

Mrs. Kelley to the Rescue

"Zero hour" for the Grange was May 1, 1868.

After six non-productive weeks on the road with weariness, hunger, and little to show for his pioneering efforts except the organization of Fredonia Grange No. 1, in Fredonia, N.Y., the always enthusiastic, courageous Kelley seemed utterly disheartened when he returned home. He even had to borrow his railroad fare from Masonic friends at Madison, Wis., to reach his farm home at Itasca, Minn. He told his wife that he had endeavored to do something worthwhile for the farmer "who was not willing even to help himself!"

Temperance Lane Kelley, unknown to her husband, had received a $500 legacy from a distant relative. She had carefully saved it in spite of the harassing situation around the impoverished farm homestead where *almost everything* was badly needed.

What she did undoubtedly saved the Grange! After hearing her husband's story she gave him the $500 along with sympathetic, but challenging words of encouragement. She urged him to try again—to continue his inspired organizational efforts.

Without this financial and inspirational aid the discouraged Kelley might never have resumed his crusade to start the Grange; and it was unlikely that any of the other Founders would have done so.

Thus did Caroline Hall, a teacher who became Kelley's assistant, and Temperance Lane Kelley, his wife, put their mark on the only family organization of its kind in the world. One Grange historian described it in these strong words: "Had the seven Founders of the Grange lacked these two encouraging women to offer frequent counseling and hope, it is doubtful that the Order of Patrons of Husbandry would have gotten much beyond the naming stage."

No. 1 in Recognizing Women

The spectacular action of the Founders in giving women full equality and a vote placed the Grange in another No. 1 leadership position. It was the first American association of any general sort—not only the first farm organization—to work for equality and justice for women.

Early sessions of the Grange declared for women suffrage and it was Grange support and influence which undoubtedly assisted greatly in bringing about equal suffrage for men and women in the United States.

This is the resolution adopted at the 1885 National Grange session:

> **Resolved,** that one of the fundamental principles of the Patrons of Husbandry, as set forth in its Declaration of Purposes, regulating membership, recognizes the equality of the two sexes. We are therefore prepared to hail with delight any advancement in the legal status of woman, which may give to her the full right of the ballot-box, and an equal condition of citizenship.

It was not until 1920, some 53 years after the Grange had established the principle of equality, that the 19th Amendment to the Constitution of the United States forbidding the states from making sex a qualification for voting, was ratified.

GRANGE LADIES PRE-SENT QUILT TO MRS. DWIGHT D. EISEN-HOWER—The wife of the President receives a prize-winning quilt at the White House. (l to r) Mrs. Beatty Dimit, Ind., Pa.; Mrs. James E. Heinly, Maiden Creek, Pa.; Mrs. C. Wesley Starr, Cheyney, Pa.; Mrs. Eisen-hower; Mrs. Herschel New-som, Washington, and Mrs. Paul W. Mitchell, Hokessin, Del. The quilt was made by Virginville, Pa., women of the Grange.

Children in the Grange

Further proof, if any is needed, of the extent to which the Grange is truly a family institution is found in its programs for children and youth.

Again, the far-sighted Founders scored! The admission of boys 14 to 16 years of age, and girls, 12 to 14, was approved nearly 100 years ago, and Anson Bartlett, of North Madison, Ohio, who early joined the Founders to help, gave this sage advice:

> There is a time in the life of every farmer's boy when he becomes disgusted with farm life. At or before that time I would admit him to the Order and try to educate him to a love of the occupation.

That children and their welfare, as well as their value through early indoctrination as future adult members, were in the thoughts of the Founders is seen also in the words of Founder Kelley when he wrote to Founder Francis M. McDowell July 27, 1868:

> I suggest having a primary degree expressly for the little folks from six or eight to sixteen years, so as to entertain and instruct the children in the rural districts and get their minds interested in the study of the beauties of Nature, as well as to afford them some rational recreation.

Again at the 1877 National Grange session, in his report as Secretary, Kelley recommended:

> Establish primary Granges for children. In these we can teach them by illustrative lessons, interspersed with music and singing, to love the farm. Give them amusement and recreation. Have in each Grange a microscope and a copy of Webster's Unabridged.

Today, the Junior Grange with its inspiring-plus-work programs, and emphasis on Subordinate Grange membership, ritual, and community service activities for youth under 16 is without equal in America. It provides broad, enlightening, satisfying, and maturing experiences leading to outstanding manhood and womanhood.

JUNIOR GRANGE OFFICERS AND DEGREE TEAM demonstrating Junior Grange work at the 99th Annual Session of the National Grange at Topeka, Kan., November, 1965.

Objectives

3

Grange Guideposts:

1. All prosperity springs from the production of wealth; or anything which retards the production of wealth is unsound.

2. The compensation of each should be based on what he contributes to the general welfare.

3. The prime purpose of government is to protect its citizens from aggression—both physical and economic.

—Albert S. Goss
(in his National Master's Address, 1942)

In the long struggle of the past 100 years to build the economy of the farmer, his community, and the nation, and to bring about equality of income opportunity for farm and rural people, the Grange has seen success after success crown its many efforts.

With the stated goal of a fuller and more rewarding country life, Grange objectives have fitted into the needs of the time—whatever they were. In all sorts of circumstances, climates, and conditions, the Grange has demonstrated a remarkable flexibility to fit itself and its pronouncements into the current situation. Today, it fits into the complex conditions of this Atomic or "Jet" Age.

In the 1860's the early Grangers found America with no adequate Department of Agriculture, no Extension Service, no agricultural education in schools, no effective agricultural press, no unified agricultural

AT DEDICATION OF GRANGE BUILDING JUNE, 1960 — President Eisenhower and Secretary of Agriculture Ezra Taft Benson with National Master Herschel D. Newsom preparing to receive officers and delegates of the National Grange following dedication ceremonies. At left, Mrs. Newsom.

program of any kind. Big business and growing cities looked upon agriculture as something to exploit. People believed there was no end to free land and soil fertility. Those who enjoy the organization of today cannot appreciate the helplessness of the farmer in those days.

Not for Farmers Alone

Over the years, as the Grange worked for the development of America in its broadest sense, its accomplishments appealed to many who came to realize that the Grange is not an organization for farmers only. Its objectives encompass national and international needs that serve and benefit all the people.

An important paragraph from the Grange's Declaration of Purposes established this primary goal:

> We desire a proper equality, equity, and fairness; protection for the weak; restraint upon the strong; in short, justly distributed burdens and justly distributed power. These are American ideals, the very essence of American independence, and to advocate the contrary is unworthy of the sons and daughters of an American Republic.

That was written nearly 100 years ago.

Today's Grange Objectives and Policies

Here in the language of today are the broad objectives of Grange action to benefit farmers, rural and urban consumers, families in the growing rur-urban areas; and Grange policies as to the national and international problems that affect all U.S. citizens:

> 1. We recognize the importance of preserving and protecting the integrity of the owner-operator-manager farm, as a guarantee to the Nation of the efficient and abundant production of high-quality food and fiber at reasonable prices for the domestic and world markets.
>
> 2. We seek to obtain for American farmers a return for their labor, management, risk and investment which bears a reasonable relationship to that received for these same economic factors in any other segment of our economy, as well as adequate compensation for their contribution to the general welfare.
>
> 3. We must develop and activate commodity programs which will give agricultural producers and workers maximum opportunities to freely exercise managerial ability and competitive advantage in cooperation with programs authorized and administered by Government, where necessary, which would operate within the framework of "freedom under law."
>
> 4. We must seek to achieve equitable income by placing major reliance upon the primary domestic market and, at the same time, maintain the influence and effect of competition and efficient production upon secondary markets; providing freedom of competition in world markets, within our treaty commitments and international responsibility.

5. We would avoid excessive dependence upon the Federal Government; but look to the Government for protection from economic aggression arising from extreme market fluctuations, caused by speculation and manipulation of market and distributive systems, which void natural competitive influences.

6. We would improve our supply and demand situation by carefully combining incentives to sound land management, with provisions for an equitable return from the primary American, and cash export markets; providing no profit, however, for producing for a market which does not exist.

7. We would maximize the benefits from the fabulous productive capacity and efficiency of American agriculture; continuing to support and improve programs to utilize the products which accrue from our economy of abundance, to relieve hunger and improve nutritional standards at home and abroad; and at the same time, seek to develop and expand domestic and foreign markets.

8. We would pursue trade policies which would avoid the destruction of jobs and the impairment of the integrity of capital at home; granting other nations the right to assume comparable responsibility to their own people and investment and, at the same time, seeking always to gain recognition that the true interests of all people of the world are to be advanced in progressively freer trade movements on a basis of competitive ability of the producer.

9. We would continue to develop and promote programs, both within and outside of government, to improve rural health and education, to improve the security of the family-type farm, to strengthen cooperatives, expand research, improve markets, strengthen rural communities, enhance rural living; in short, to do everything prudent and reasonable to protect and enhance the efficiency, the productive capacity, the human dignity, the economic freedom of those who produce our food and fiber; that they may have an equitable share of the wealth that they create, and enjoy the blessings which will accrue in a balanced economic society.

10. We would provide protection against excessive losses to producers due to unforeseen and unavoidable causes; thereby promoting economic stability in America and, at the same time assure that food needs of the Nation are met.

FFA YOUTH MEET GRANGE MASTER—Each year youth leaders of the Future Farmers of America come to Grange headquarters in Washington to learn more about Grange activities and goals. The event signifies Grange emphasis on potential leadership in rural life.

4

1966-67
Centennial Activities

The Centennial Year will be one of the greatest Grange and Patron activity, on top of the regularly-scheduled Subordinate, Pomona, State and National programs which are extensive in themselves each year. The special Centennial events will make an even busier year than usual for Officers and members, as well as filling each with new satisfactions, new joy, and new realization of the justifiably important national and international position and prestige attained by the Grange—truly a broad and genuine base for pride in membership.

The Grange Family Meditation Center and Chapel at Gettysburg, Pa.

As a lasting reminder to the nation of the first 100 years of the Grange, there will be erected at the National Soldiers Cemetery at Gettysburg, Pa., the *Grange Family Meditation Center and Chapel.*

This beautiful edifice, to be available for use by families or groups in connection with all types of ceremonies at the Cemetery, is an appropriate development at this Grange Centennial time!

Patrons will recall the great contribution that William Saunders, one of the Founders and the first National Master, made to the establishment of the Grange and to its early formative years.

One hundred years ago he was Superintendent of the Propagating Gardens of the United States Department of Agriculture. His office was a small brick building on the corner of Missouri Avenue and 3½ Street, Washington, D.C. This became the first meeting place of the Grange Founders.

The Centennial Committee

Chairman: William J. Brake, Lecturer, National Grange, 5875 Montebello Avenue, Haslett, Mich.

Mrs. Sherman K. (Lida) Ives, Rt. 1, Morris, Connecticut

Mrs. Everett A. (Dorothy) Willard, Rt. 1, Newsport, Vermont

Matthias E. Smith, President, Farmers and Traders Life Ins. Co., 960 James Street, Syracuse, New York

Kenneth P. Colby, Exec. Vice Pres., National Grange Mutual Ins. Co., Keene, New Hampshire

C. Dana Bennett, Foundation for American Agriculture, 1425 H Street, N.W., Washington, D.C.

Henry Roberts, President, Grange Mutual Life Company, Nampa, Idaho

Mrs. James W. (Agnes) Ingwersen, Junior Grange Superintendent, Rt. 2, LeRoy, Kansas

William J. Van Horn, President, Grange Insurance Association, 2717 3rd Avenue, Seattle, Washington

Herschel D. Newsom, National Master, The National Grange, 1616 H Street, N.W., Washington, D.C.

Consultant to the Centennial Committee: Dr. Raymond W. Miller, 1005 Dupont Circle Building, Washington, D.C.

National Master Saunders was an outstanding landscape architect, and when the National Cemetery at Gettysburg was conceived, he was called to the task of planning it. At President Abraham Lincoln's request he spent an evening at the White House going over the entire proposed layout. The President enthusiastically approved Mr. Saunders' recommendations, and early in October, 1863, interments began. Mr. Saunders was formally thanked by the Government, and received the personal thanks of President Lincoln for his great work.

Thus, it is appropriate that his name be linked with the Grange in the erection of this Memorial Meditation Center which will be dedicated on November 12, 1967, by Grange officers and thousands of members.

Plan Conceived by Alvin E. Hanson

The idea for this Family Meditation Center and Chapel was originally conceived and promoted by Alvin E. Hanson, late president of the Farmers and Traders Life Insurance Company, of Syracuse, N.Y.

As one of the original members of the Grange Centennial Celebration Committee, Mr. Hanson visited Gettysburg Cemetery. He was inspired to suggest that the Grange seek authorization from the U.S. Department of Interior to erect a suitable memorial to Mr. Saunders as one of the Centennial projects.

Mr. Hanson had studied, in the Grange Memorial Library in Washington, D.C., the hand-written Memoirs of Mr. Saunders "relating to my participation in the planning, and installing of the soldiers National Cemetery at Gettysburg." The details of Mr. Saunders' development of the cemetery plans intrigued Mr. Hanson, as did President Lincoln's personal interest in the topography of the area. Mr. Saunders related how he was invited to the dedication ceremony, and sat on the platform when the President delivered his famous address.

Mr. Hanson's dream was to have the Family Meditation Center and Chapel built in time for the Centennial observance. The Centennial Committee obtained approval from the U. S. Department of Interior to erect such a memorial, subject to the Department's approval of the final architectural plans for the structure.

On Mr. Hanson's untimely passing in December, 1965, his associates led by the then Executive Vice President Matthias E. Smith, now President, of the Farmers and Traders Life Insurance Company, pledged that they would work closely with the Grange in carrying to completion the product of Mr. Hanson's ideas.

Law Essay Contest

Another Grange Centennial feature has been the preparation by law students of papers explaining the origin and history of the Granger Laws and their significance. Title of the National Contest sponsored by the Grange to obtain the cooperation of the certified law schools of the country was "The Impact of the Grange on Social Legislation." (See Chapter 6).

The National Master and the Centennial Committee were greatly aided in developing rules for this contest, as well as procedures for properly announcing and conducting it, by a distinguished Advisory Committee of Law School Administrators:

Vernon X. Miller, Dean, School of Law, The Catholic University of America, Washington, D. C.

Clarence Clyde Ferguson, Jr., Dean, School of Law, Howard University, Washington, D. C.

B. J. Tennery, Associate Dean, Washington College of Law, The American University, Washington, D. C.

Richard Alan Gordon, Assistant Dean, Georgetown University Law Center, Washington, D. C.

Charles B. Nutting, Administrator, National Law Center, The George Washington University, Washington, D. C.

John G. Hervey, Dean, School of Law, Oklahoma City University, Advisor to Council, Section of Legal Education and Admission to the Bar, American Bar Association, Oklahoma City, Okla.

Members of the Board of Judges:

Judge Thurman Wesley Arnold, former Assistant Attorney General of the United States, in charge of Anti-Trust; for five years Associate Justice, U.S. Court of Appeals Washington, D. C.

Dr. Robert E. Goostree, Professor of Law, American University, Washington, D. C.

Father (Dr.) Joseph M. Snee, Professor of Law, Georgetown University, Washington, D. C.

Following announcement in November, 1966, of the winners of the $1000, $500, and $250 awards, the National Grange will publish these outstanding winning essays, as another Centennial feature.

Grange Caravan

The Grange Caravan is expected to include thousands of Grange members in a motorcade pilgrimage to the Nation's Capital, thence from Washington, D.C. to Gettysburg and on to Syracuse, N.Y. for the 101st Centennial Sessions of the National Grange opening on Monday, November 13, 1967.

Included in plans for the huge "celebration" will be special events in Washington, D.C. on November 10 and 11, 1967; the dedication of the Grange Family Meditation Center and Chapel at Gettysburg on Novem-12, the full-scale meetings as well as Degree work at Syracuse. It is expected that the Seventh Degree will be conferred there on the greatest number of candidates ever assembled at a Grange session.

Among the additional Centennial projects are the:

Centennial Playwriting Contest

Conceived to provide plays to be used by Granges during the Centennial Year, this contest is sponsored by the Farmers and Traders Life Insurance Company, through the Lecturers Department.

Judging will be at the 1966 National Grange Session.

Centennial Songwriting Contest

This contest has been under way for several years. The ten best of each of the two classifications as selected by the judges each year will be eligible for the finals to be held at the 1966 National Grange Sessions.

U.S. 5c Centennial Postage Stamp

The design, consisting of a rural scene in the background with the Grange emblem super-imposed in foreground has been approved. The first issue of this 5c postage stamp is planned for the centennial year.

The Grange 1867-1967—First Century of Service and Evolution

In compliance with my assignment from the Centennial Committee to prepare this 128-page booklet briefly summarizing the "First Century of Service and Evolution," it becomes crystal clear that there is a wealth of important material and information available in various libraries, including the Grange Memorial Library in the Nation's Capital, to make a highly significant, comprehensive history of the Grange for this 100 years which will close, as this Centennial Celebration itself comes to a climax—in November, 1967.

Listing of Grange Monuments and Markers

This appropriate activity to build the "bank" of historical information about the Grange is being developed through the Grange Lecturers across the nation. Such information will prove of great value in development of another Centennial project to come in the next few years—the Comprehensive Grange History.

Comprehensive Century History

This will be a detailed history of the first 100 years of the Grange. Publication date is planned after the Centennial Year to encompass the full 100 years of Grange service. In connection with this, a plan is being developed to collect and safeguard Grange historical material, including preservation of historical material in Subordinate Granges in Archives and indexing of this material utilizing a specially-designed uniform indexing system so that all of the local material will be indexed in the same way for convenient reference. It is also planned that a pamphlet be prepared and distributed so that Grangers may be able to recognize and help preserve these historical materials.

Rebirth of National Grange Monthly Magazine

With evidence mounting of the need to improve communications within the Grange, to furnish more information to all members, to stimulate better discussions, and to reach influential nonmembers whose understanding and support are essential, the last Grange Annual Session voted to reactivate the official *National Grange Monthly Magazine*, thus adding a very significant feature to the Grange Centennial Program.

Its first issue will inaugurate the Centennnial Year in November, 1966, and appear just ahead of the 100th Annual Session.

This reactivated publication will help build a closer relationship between members and the national unit of their Grange, and will carry on the traditions of the early *Grange Weekly* and the late *Monthly* that were strong, progressive, and vigorous advocates of Grange principles, and live exponents of the policies and national activities of the Grange.

Early in this century, when Vol. 1, No. 1 of the first Grange publication was started, the then National Master made this comment, which is as true today:

> We are cognizant of the tremendous responsibility attached to the establishment and maintenance of a paper, national in scope, and representing an organization as this paper will represent, but the possibilities in such an undertaking are so great that we enter upon the task without hesitancy.

CENTENNIAL HEADQUARTERS — The Grange Building, near the White House and Lafayette Square, will be the focal point of the Centennial observance, and will be visited by thousands of Grange members and others throughout the year. (See interior photos on Page 24.)

II

Origin of the Patrons of Husbandry 1867

"In its origin the Order of Patrons of Husbandry was a *pro-vidential creation:* a statement at once so startling, so unusual and so easily suggestive of actual irreverence, that it should not be made by anyone unless capable of complete verification by positive facts.

"Of the truth of its assertion there is not the slightest question, when one has closely examined the conditions out of which the Order had its inception, and the objects which it was not only created to accomplish, but has actually accomplished . . ."

—*Grange Historian* CHARLES M. GARDNER

OUTSTANDING Grange Memorial Library on 10th floor of Grange Headquarters building, Washington, D.C. Contains valuable historic and irreplaceable books, and reports on Grange activities, including the Personal Library of William Saunders, first National Master.

BEAUTIFUL—but functional Agricultural Conference Room which is a memorial to National Master Albert S. Goss, on the ground floor of Grange Headquarters Building. Master Goss was an outstanding advocate of the conference method of reconciling differences and achieving a common understanding and goal. This room is regularly used by many non-governmental groups in the Nation's Capital as a convenient meeting place.

5 Conditions Leading to Organization of the Grange

The American today can scarcely appreciate, or hardly believe, the life of the farmer and rural resident of 100 years ago. No lights, no radio, no telephone, no television, no truck or automobile on every farm, few paved roads, no easy communication with others. Little, if any, social life. Discouragement, and an ever-present sense of futility. No way out of an isolated existence fast becoming intolerable.

1867 was a troublesome period of reconstruction following the War Between the States. Abraham Lincoln was gone. President Andrew Johnson was seeking to cope with serious political, social, and economic problems.

Charles M. Gardner, Massachusetts State Master, and for 35 years Managing Editor of the *National Grange Monthly,* in his book *The Grange—Friend of the Farmer,* paints a vivid picture of the conditions that led to the founding of the Grange. Some excerpts:

We of today cannot grasp the magnitude of the reconstruction problem that faced this country immediately following the close of the war.

These facts became immediately apparent as the reconstruction problem was faced:

1. That reconstruction would be a slow, uphill process which nothing short of many years could accomplish.
2. That it was a task in which every citizen's assistance was needed, exercised through both individual and organized channels, to the extreme limit of opportunity.
3. That facilities must be provided, both North and South, for candid discussion of the issues involved; and with a constant effort both sides of the line toward mutual tolerance, forgiveness, and cooperation.

Into this situation the Order of Patrons of Husbandry was born, a providential creation because it was called into being at a time of particular need to perform work imperatively demanded; a task, which by its very nature, such an organization was admirably fitted to meet.

The close of the Civil War found industries prostrate, agriculture with the rest, and it was immediately apparent that unless that fundamental occupation could be speedily revived, the fertility of neglected fields restored, and the food supply of a nation promptly increased to normal proportions, then all other industry would languish, and the future if not the very life, of the whole people would be menaced.

All the government machinery in existence was therefore set at work on this problem, which was easily seen to lie at the very base of the reconstruction task, and into this undertaking entered Oliver Hudson Kelley and his associates as active factors. Here was conceived the great necessity for which the Grange was destined to be an effective solution; and here was providential creation, worked out—as so often has happened in the history of world affairs—through humble human agency, but successful because possessed of large vision and prompted by sincere motives.

Farmer Unrest Follows War

Prof. Solon Justus Buck, with connections at the University of Illinois and Harvard University, has told a clear and comprehensive story of the situation in his book *The Granger Movement—A Study of Agricultural Organization and Its Political, Economic and Social Manifestations, 1870-1880.* Published in 1913 (and republished in 1965 by University of Nebraska Press), the 384-page book is considered an authority on the subject and on the extremely important role of the Grange.

In the decade following the Civil War, farmers believed they were not advancing as rapidly as others.

While farmers in the Northeastern part of the United States had dairying and market gardening, hay, potatoes, and fruit giving many profitable employments, other parts of the country were not so fortunate.

The South was left by the war in a state of complete exhaustion in which agriculture shared to the fullest extent; farms had been destroyed or often the owners had been killed in battle and most of all the complete change in the industrial system made a return to normal agricultural conditions extremely slow.

The great prairie states of the upper Mississippi Valley from Ohio to Kansas and Nebraska, producers of wheat and corn, were the center of agricultural discontent. It was there that the protective movement among the farmers manifested itself most vigorously. The moving westward of the wheat industry was leaving these states with discontented farmers facing depreciation in land values and finding it necessary to turn to stock raising and dairy farming. Burdened with debt and also despairing, they put the blame on bankers, railroads, legislation, tariff, and monopolies. While some of their grievances had been caused by their own shortcomings, many of their grievances were well-founded.

Grievances Against Railroads Grow

Their grievance against the railroads, treated in Chapter 6, was twofold. Many unsuspecting farmers lost every penny as they were victimized by unscrupulous brokers who sold them stock in new rail lines. Secondly, railroad rates, management, and service were uncontrolled and discrimination was practiced in fixing the rates.

Again farmers felt, that as a class, they failed to receive adequate representation in the Government. They felt that their interests were not given due consideration by those who were supposed to represent them.

The 43rd Congress of the United States (1873-1875), furnishes an example. Sixty-one percent of the members were lawyers, 16 percent were engaged in commercial pursuits, and only seven percent were farmers. However, the census of 1870 showed that 47 percent of the working public was still engaged in farming, while commerce and manufacturing could claim only 31 percent.

Usually ignorant of market conditions and of the laws of supply and demand, and with no facilities for storing their crops, farmers often were forced into selling their products in a glutted market. They received small return for their hard, careful work. The wrath of the farmers was also directed against commission merchants through whom they were forced to dispose of their crops at quite unremunerative prices.

For example, a common story in the *Proceedings* of the Illinois State Grange in 1875 told of a farmer carrying a load of grain to market and returning with a pair of shoes for his boy—the sole purchase which he was able to make from the proceeds of the sale of his grain.

Among farmers there was general poverty and a widespread indebtedness as represented by the growing burden of mortgages, often at excessive rates of interest. Loan agents infested the West. Sometimes interest on loans ran as high as 15 or 20 percent.

Following the War, various conditions brought about substantial decreases in the prices farmers received. Their decreasing income and increasing costs led to serious personal situations.

These, then, were the conditions which led to the organization and early building of the Grange. As Buck concluded:

> An agricultural organization including a great part of the farmers of the nation, would be able to demand fairer treatment from the railway corporations and to enforce it with the help of the state; it could use its immense influence to secure more favorable legislation on such matters as the tariff, currency, and taxation; by means of a widespread local organization it could gather and disseminate useful information concerning the crops and the markets; and in general it could foster a beneficent spirit of cooperation and mutual assistance among its members. In this way alone can a satisfactory explanation be found for the widespread and phenomenal movement for organization which appeared among the farmers in the decade of the seventies.

Even as the Patrons of Husbandry in 1867 was so well designed and fitted to meet the problems of that day, so in 1966 are the Patrons of Husbandry (Grange members) equally capable, in the words of the National Master at the 1965 Annual Meeting, "in meeting and dealing with the problems of this day."

"We must enter now into a new and broader series of effective, constructive, and intelligent adjustments, made necessary by new and rapidly developing interrelationships and interdependence with increasing numbers of people throughout the entire world."

6

The Granger
Laws —
Their Significance

"The created is never greater than the creator."
—Grange slogan

So profound an impact have the "Granger Laws" had on modifying—
and improving—the American service capitalistic system that every law
student since 1873 has been required to learn how they came about, and
their significance in building protection, and in requiring fair treatment,
for every citizen from public utilities, thus helping to make the United
States the world power it is today.

As an important feature of the Grange Centennial observance, students
in U.S. accredited law schools were invited in 1965 to compete in a national contest by analyzing and writing about "The Impact of the Grange
on Social Legislation," with particular reference to the Granger Laws.

In the announcement of this timely contest to spotlight, nearly 100 years
later, this far-reaching accomplishment of the Grange, it was explained
that:

> The fundamental concept in government-business relations in our nation
> flows from Granger Laws. Under them, monopolistic tendencies of capitalistic
> business have been controlled by regulatory laws so as to preserve the benefits
> of competitive enterprise, the ingenuity of man and human dignity, and still
> have the benefits of large-scale production from the incentive of free men.
>
> During the same approximate period of time that America has become the
> production marvel of the world, much of the world, because of the frustrations
> engendered by monopolistic practices of cartels and predatory trusts, has been
> encouraged to take the road to state capitalism as part of dictatorial, materialistic
> communism.
>
> The National Grange, as part of its 100th anniversary in 1967, feels obligated
> to encourage the present-day law student to become familiar with the origin and
> history of these Granger Laws, the first of which were declared constitutional in
> 1876 (in Munn vs. Illinois). Subsequent decisions have permitted a greatly
> expanded scope of regulation to preserve private ownership and protect it
> against monopoly or state socialism. The impact and significance of this social
> legislation is the theme of the contest.

How the Granger Movement Started

In 1873, when the first regular delegate session of the National Grange held in Georgetown, Washington, D. C., brought together representatives of 11 states, the most important question demanding attention was that of *monopolies*, chiefly in transportation.

Today's citizens, conscious of the established powers of the Interstate Commerce Commission to regulate rates, determine rules and procedures for interstate shipments by rail or truck, and require adherence to performance and safety standards, can hardly realize the situation in the 1860's.

In his classic book, *The Granger Movement*, Solon Justice Buck traced the fundamental conditions that brought about the early growth of the Grange, and the Granger Movement which has been such an important factor in America's progress.

In carefully researched terms with many citations of origin, Prof. Buck sets the stage:

Previous to about 1870 there was little thought of public control of railways: they were looked upon as blessings to the country, the extension of which should be encouraged, rather than checked by subjecting them to interference. It was generally supposed that competition would prove an efficient regulator, and so the demand was for more railroads and hence more competition rather than for governmental regulation.

During the period of railway expansion that followed the war, however, it began to be evident that competition was not going to curb the power of the railroad corporations because of the ease with which consolidations were effected.

Agreements between the various trunk lines for the maintenance of rates, made necessary by the ruinous rate wars, were also frequent during this period, and nothing could serve better to arouse the anger of the farmers and rural politicians than the thought of two or three railroad magnates meeting together and agreeing to maintain a certain rate or, as they put it, to impose an additional tax on the products of agricultural labor. . . .

There were many things in the management of railroads in the early seventies which tended to arouse antagonism on the part not only of the farmers but of the public in general.

. . . they denied the right of the public, the states, or the nation to regulate or in any way interfere with their operations. There seems to have been, also, a general disregard of the convenience of customers on the part of railway officials and employees. Travelers and shippers are said to have been subjected to all sorts of discourtesies and even injuries and any attempt to secure justice was apt to result in persecutions by the powerful corporation.

. . . Complaint was also made of the influence which was exercised by the railroad corporations over legislators and public officials. The most prevalent form of this influence was the free pass system . . .

It was in the shape of rates or tariffs, however, that the railroad problem was most closely brought home to the farmer. The charges preferred were that railroad rates in general were too high and that gross discrimination was practiced in fixing them. When the Iowa farmer was burning corn for fuel, because at fifteen cents a bushel it was cheaper than coal, while at the same time it was selling for a dollar in the East, he felt that there was something wrong and quite naturally accused the railroads of extortion. . . .

It is quite evident then that the farmers had a number of real grievances against the railroads, although they did not always clearly understand the situation or realize just where the trouble lay.

It was in the four northwestern states of Illinois, Minnesota, Iowa, and Wisconsin that the most important railroad restrictive laws were enacted; and in these states arose the principal cases leading to important judicial decisions. Here, too, were the states with the strongest Grange influence, which was the principal force back of the movement for railroad regulation.

However, Grange influence and demand for restrictive legislation was not confined to these states. In almost every state there arose demand for regulation, with the Patrons of Husbandry in the forefront of the agitation.

Buck credits the Grange in his summary in these words: ". . . It is not too much to say that the fundamental principles upon which American regulation of railroads by legislation has developed were first worked out in the Granger states of the Northwest during the decade of the seventies."

The Granger Laws and the Supreme Court

Perhaps the most important results of the state-by-state Grange fight for railroad legislation was the action of the United States Supreme Court in handing down decisions in seven Granger cases in November, 1876. These decisions established the fundamental principle that the state has the right to regulate monopolies.

Vital Principle Established by Grange Fight

The distinctive slogan of Grange origin in the great fight was *"the created is never greater than the creator."*

Using this slogan as the basic argument for the regulatory legislation, the favorable court decisions established the fundamental principle that the state which permitted the monopoly retained unto itself the right to regulate and control that monopoly.

Federal Legislation Follows Same Principle

When it became apparent that individual state legislation could not solve the problems created by the situation in transportation, the principle previously upheld in the state courts was applied on the national level in the passage in 1887 of the Interstate Commerce Act. Later legislation applied this principle of monopoly control to all public utilities, as well as franchised operations permitted under federal law.

The problem of the development of monopolies and cartels in the rest of the economy was confronted by passage of the Sherman Antitrust Act in 1890. Instead of regulating their action and rates as had been done with the railroads and public utilities, it provided that the self-regulating features of the competitive market should be preserved by the prevention of monopolies and other practices which operated to restrain trade or destroy competition.

The adoption of these two laws which were the heart of the Granger legislation became one of the landmarks of economic history. The modified capitalistic system which developed in the United States under the guidelines of these progressive laws avoided the errors which had developed in Eastern European capitalism, which made their system vulnerable to socialism.

Thus, the regulation of monopolies and the preservation of the competitive system in the U.S. has resulted in the greatest economic development, the widest ownership of production, the most liberal distribution of profits, and the highest standard of living of any major country of the world. Without the Granger Laws this would not have been possible, and indeed, the U.S. might well be a socialistic nation today.

Since these historic beginnings, the same principles have been applied to communications, air transportation, and the regulation of commodity and stock exchanges.

The Grange still considers the Government a partner in the preservation of a competitive market where possible, and in the operation of a regulated market where necessary. This concept of the relationship of Government to the economic life of our country was restated by the National Grange in 1942 when it established as a part of its policies three guideposts for the solution of present-day economic problems. One was:

"The prime purpose of government is to protect its citizens from aggression—both physical and economic."

The Granger Movement is not dead. It is still at the center of our economic life. Its contribution is immeasurable; its future is as certain as the democracy of which it is so much a part.

GRANGE VIEWS ARE HEARD—President Lyndon B. Johnson listens as Grange Legislative Representative Harry Graham, Legislative Counsel Joseph O. Parker, and National Master Herschel D. Newsom explain Grange positions on farm and rural problems.

Evolution of Grange Legislative Program and Positions

7

For the Welfare of All

With nearly 100 years of non-partisan national legislative accomplishments behind it, the Grange starts its second century endorsing, urging, and supporting every well-conceived proposition for the educational, social, and economic betterment of agricultural people, as well as for the welfare of all U.S. citizens.

Not organized originally for political reasons, or to become a powerful legislative force, these aims not being in the minds of the Founders 100 years ago, nevertheless the Grange has become one of the most potent influences in the nation's capital, and commands the attention of administrators and others prominent in the Executive branch of government, as well as of lawmakers both in Congress and in state capitals.

The national headquarters of the Grange in Washington utilizes a legislative representative in addition to a legislative counsel and an associate legislative counsel, all working under the direction of the National Master who likewise gives a great deal of his personal attention to legislative matters. Thus these four, together with the national transportation counsel in the Grange office, become the eyes and ears of Grange membership and of rural and suburban Americans. It has been heartening and encouraging in recent years to observe the continuing improvement in response from Grange leaders all across the country to requests from their national office to make their views known with reference to official Grange policy.

Meanwhile, these five experienced, well-informed official spokesmen, aided by other staff associates, are advocates or exponents of Grange policy and position. They give careful scrutiny to all legislative proposals with national or international implications which may have an effect on the lives and fortunes of the rural citizens of the country. The Grange Master and the special representatives speak up—for—or against—as need be and as may be directed by the delegate body, which has acted in annual meeting to spell out what the Grange position should be.

First appointed in 1878, a National Grange Legislative Committee became the pioneering, organized effort to properly represent the rural interests of the country. Prior to that, actions of the Founders and of the first National Masters to represent Grange interests were somewhat spasmodic. Grange Historian Charles M. Gardner's studies indicated that

PRESIDENT KENNEDY signing Grange-supported Wheat-Cotton Bill of 1963— presenting pen to House Agriculture Chairman Harold D. Cooley. Senate Agriculture Chairman Allen J. Ellender admires his souvenir pen at right, with Vice President Johnson, Senate Leader Humphrey, Secretary Freeman, and National Grange Master Newsom looking on.

Grange influence was thrown only for or against specific measures pending in Congress, in which agricultural interests were involved. He continued:

> Extensive as Kelley's dream of future Grange usefulness may have been, it is extremely doubtful whether he ever visualized how powerful a legislative force the organization was destined to become. To the Founders, the primary objective was a more satisfying rural life and a happier farm home.

To Grange leaders over the past 25 years, it has become increasingly evident that the Grange must assume a major responsibility *for providing a national balance* in public affairs by giving to rural Americans and farmers the most effective voice and advocacy that it can possibly give to balance increasingly *big* business, *big* labor, and *big* government. *But true balance there must be.* Grange members can be proud of the efforts of their organization toward achieving this balance. The Grange leaders readily admit that much remains to be done—especially in the field of building a sound public opinion through more effective information.

What was said 50 years ago, at the Golden Jubilee celebration of the National Grange, can be said with even greater force today, as the record of Grange legislative accomplishment is outstanding, and the aims and objectives continue in the same vein:

> No well-informed person would claim that the Grange is wholly responsible for all of these agricultural achievements, but that it has been an important, and, in many instances, the dominating factor in bringing them about, no one but the uninformed will deny. Upon all movements for rural betterment, the Grange, through its perfect and well-disciplined machinery, has been a leader in creating that public opinion which has influenced Congress, legislators and courts, and has shaken to its foundations the old, circumscribed, aristocratic idea of education and broadened our social and economic views. . . .
>
> It was a widespread opinion in the early years of the Grange movement that the farmers were not represented in our law-making bodies as they should be and that their interests were neglected or discriminated against. The Grange has done what it could without breaking into partisan politics to stem the tide that has been setting against the farmers as an important factor in our governing citizenship. . . .

Today, as it was in 1919 when Legislative Headquarters were first opened in Washington, D.C., the sound policy of the Grange has been to present its viewpoints and arguments for or against legislative proposals to Committees of Congress and to the White House and Executive Departments on a high plane. The activity includes no "lobby"—Grange action is through conferences with members of Congress in committee rooms or offices. Very often, Grange viewpoints are invited, with the National Master or his staff meeting with legislators at their request to provide first-hand information.

While other farm and commodity groups in Washington are very active and possess extensive influence, it is the general opinion that the cause of the real "dirt farmer" and "rural life" is most truly represented by the Grange.

How Grange Policy Is Determined

One important reason is that thousands of Grange members literally meet thousands of times annually and engage in extensive discussion on legislative matters to determine what Grange policy should be, and what they will do as citizens and voters to back the Grange legislative program.

Before effective action can be taken in regard to any matter, the sentiment of Grange members must be crystallized, their differences reconciled, and support or opposition to a pending legislative matter must be decided. Often, through this process, legislative proposals themselves are *generated.*

The unique machinery of the Grange is well-adapted to this. Views expressed and resolutions adopted by Subordinate and Pomona Granges are further considered by the State Granges, and from there sent for action to the National Grange annual meeting.

At these annual sessions, literally hundreds of resolutions on important legislative items are discussed before the policy of the Grange is finally determined. These are serious and some might say, tedious sessions, but the results have proved their value.

In these published words of a State Master describing what happened at a recent session is dramatic proof of the thoroughness of Grange procedure:

> The National Grange session was definitely not a play session. More than 400 resolutions were considered covering many areas not all directly connected with the farm, but covering a wide range of things important to people throughout not only this nation, but the entire world.
>
> One could not help but notice the earnest dedication of the delegates as they often worked in committees far into the night drafting resolutions to be considered by the entire delegate body. Because of the widespread area represented, several issues were hotly contested.

The Grange thus provides each member with a voice—an opportunity starting in the Subordinate unit to express his beliefs and viewpoints knowing full well that his worthy ideas and recommendations may reach through Grange channels to the highest levels of the Grange and subsequently to government, with far-reaching effects on millions of U.S. citizens, as well as peoples abroad.

The Granger Laws and Farm Credit

Grange histories reveal an amazing collection of beneficial legislative achievements from which the entire population of the country—urban

PRESIDENT EISENHOWER SIGNING THE FARM CREDIT ACT OF 1953—with members of the Joint Farm Credit Committee, made up of farm and credit agencies. National Master Albert S. Goss, and subsequently National Master Herschel D. Newsom, served as Chairmen of this Joint Farm Credit Committee of Farm Organizations for some 18 years.

and rural—has profited. Many of the accomplishments were Grange-originated; others succeeded through strong Grange backing and support.

Only a few can be mentioned here due to space limitations—and the record is constantly being added to as daily legislative efforts succeed.

Outstanding among accomplishments of the Patrons of Husbandry were the actions that led to the evolution of the Granger Laws. Beginning in the 1870's, this Grange accomplishment is described in detail in Chapter 6, "The Granger Laws—Their Significance." This Granger Movement itself changed the Constitution of the United States, as was pointed out in the February, 1964, issue of *American Heritage:*

> Not a literal change involving amendments, it was on the contrary, a more important one in that for the first time in the history of the world, the courts of the United States, including the Supreme Court, recognized officially that the public does have a proper interest in the policy and decisions of big business.

Another far-reaching legislative accomplishment is in the field of farm credit. Actually the Grange developed the original Farm Credit Act and played a prominent role in the legislation that followed it for a number of years and which gave farmers control and ownership of what is now the widespread farm credit system.

It was in 1913 that National Master Oliver Wilson was the first to outline a system that "should make it easy and safe for a farmer to borrow money to buy or improve his land or the equivalent to operate same." He significantly added, "Any credit system to be safe for the people must be either directed, controlled or operated by the Government." When the first Federal Farm Loan Act was passed in 1916, it was substantially in the form suggested and advocated by the Grange. Following later was the "Land Mortgage System" and, based upon Grange recommendations, the setting up in 1933 by President Roosevelt of the Farm Credit Administration. All of this has probably done as much economically for farm people as any single group of achievements, farmers obtaining through these developments an equal opportunity for credit on fair terms. Today, the cooperative farm credit system is the envy of the world in terms of its ownership by agricultural people and the service it performs for them.

Outstanding Accomplishments in Many Other Areas

Among other legislative accomplishments of the Grange are the following:

Since 1867 it has been a "mainstay" for *rural roads* . . . a dominant force in passing legislation providing for Interstate Highway Programs now under way.

❖ ❖ ❖ ❖ ❖

Fostered creation of the *Extension Service* . . . and has consistently supported appropriations necessary to meet expanded needs of the Service.

❖ ❖ ❖ ❖ ❖

Fathered legislation *creating the Vo-Ag program*—and consistently supported advancement of the work since it was established in 1916.

❖ ❖ ❖ ❖ ❖

Initiated legislation which *removed the federal tax on fuel for "on-the-farm" use*—saving farmers some $100 million annually.

❖ ❖ ❖ ❖ ❖

Won its fight to preserve *trip leasing privileges in agricultural trucking, saving rural people $200 million a year.*

❖ ❖ ❖ ❖ ❖

Was solely responsible for initiation of Rural Free Delivery and our Parcel Post System.

❖ ❖ ❖ ❖ ❖

Led the fight that gave Cabinet status to the U.S. Department of Agriculture, and has been a stalwart supporter ever since.

❖ ❖ ❖ ❖ ❖

Laid the original groundwork for and *actually built over the years farmer cooperatives, which it strongly supports today.*

❖ ❖ ❖ ❖ ❖

Is noted far and wide for its vigilant efforts to *curb and control monopolies*, and thereby extend opportunities to more and more Americans.

❖ ❖ ❖ ❖ ❖

Sponsored legislation which *created the Rural Electrification Administration and the rural telephone program, and takes a prime interest* every year in adequate appropriations for these programs.

❖ ❖ ❖ ❖ ❖

Secured initial legislation establishing our system of *agriculture experiment stations* and has since helped Congress guide and support an adequate program of research.

✦ ✦ ✦ ✦ ✦

Championed the Soil Conservation Service, Farmers Home Administration, Crop Insurance Program, Upstream Small Watershed Program, School Lunch and Milk Program, Great Plains Program, Rural Area Development, Food for Peace Programs, now frequently taken for granted.

✦ ✦ ✦ ✦ ✦

Was the dominant force in bringing Social Security to farmers and other self-employed persons.

✦ ✦ ✦ ✦ ✦

Has consistently promoted sound money and tax policies.

✦ ✦ ✦ ✦ ✦

Played a paramount and continuing role in the *formation and operation of United Nation's Food and Agriculture Organization and of the International Federation of Agricultural Producers.*

✦ ✦ ✦ ✦ ✦

Worked aggressively and effectively for *expansion of markets for food and fiber, both at home and abroad.*

✦ ✦ ✦ ✦ ✦

Has repeatedly pushed—with success—for *tariff and trade barrier reforms.*

✦ ✦ ✦ ✦ ✦

Initiated the equality of income, or *parity concept* for measuring agricultural welfare—(and justice)—and has consistently supported modifications necessary to modernize the formula.

Groundwork for the Future

The National Master in his address at both the 1964 and 1965 annual sessions, from his vantage point of reviewing today's complex national and international situation, has laid the groundwork for legislative accomplishments leading into the Grange's second century. He has said:

> We must recognize that the problems of relationships among the people within the United States are now being substantially influenced and, indeed, in many cases magnified by the hopes and the aspirations—by the technical, social, economic and political developments around this vast but rapidly shrinking globe upon which we live, and by the very substantial evolution in transportation, communication, and commercial relations among peoples and nations.
>
> Even as the Grange in its beginning was peculiarly well designed and equipped to meet the problems of nine decades ago, so must we now be sure, that the Order of Patrons of Husbandry is equally capable of meeting and dealing with the problems, as we round out the Grange's first century, as we enter into a new and broader series of effective, constructive and intelligent adjustments, made necessary by new and rapidly developing interrelationships and interdependence with increasing numbers of people throughout the entire world.
>
> Is it now crystal clear, from the experiences within the lifetime of many of us today, that *we cannot isolate ourselves from the military and political problems of the rest of the world?*
>
> Does it not then logically follow that *we must recognize the impossibility of insulating ourselves from the food and agricultural, health, and nutritional,* as well as *economic and social problems therein?*

8

Pioneer
Granges

While literally hundreds of pioneer Granges throughout the country will be celebrating 100 years of service to their membership and community within the next few years, and their officers will be planning a suitable local observance, a bit more attention must be given to the first three Granges: the "tryout" Grange—Potomac Grange No. 1, organized in Washington, D. C., January 8, 1868; Fredonia Grange No. 1, Fredonia, Chautauqua County, N. Y., April 16, 1868; and Green Mountain Grange No. 1, St. Johnsbury, Vt., July 4, 1871.

Potomac No. 1

At the beginning, Founders of the new fraternity realized that they must have a "tryout" Grange to help in preparation of ritual and to rehearse the various degrees in an atmosphere of realism. So Potomac Grange No. 1 was designed primarily as a school of instruction. The degree work was repeated and improved and other steps taken to try out various Grange procedures. Its first Master was William M. Ireland, one of the Founders.

This Grange No. 1 served its purpose very well, but after the ritualistic features of the Grange were perfected there seemed little need for it, so it became dormant for a number of years.

Nearly 20 years later, in 1886, it was decided to reorganize it not as a "practice" Grange this time, but as an actual working Grange on exactly the same basis as those which had mushroomed throughout the country in rural areas.

Reorganized through the help and interest of two of the principal Founders, John R. Thompson and William Saunders, and relatives of other Founders, the second Potomac Grange lasted two years. The third reorganization of Potomac Grange came after an interim of 36 years. During the past more than 40 years, however, Potomac Grange has had great value and usefulness to the whole National Grange structure as well as to National Masters and their staffs, and through them to the delegate body of the National Grange in particular.

39

Two excellent purposes were behind this third reorganization in 1924. First, to bring to leaders of public opinion, including government officials, direct contact with Grange ideas of rural needs; and second, to give wide publicity to many pending public questions through Grange discussion of official viewpoints direct from their source.

Since its third reorganization, Potomac Grange has served these extremely useful purposes through its instructive and entertaining meetings. Some of the most prominent leaders in national life not only have been on the membership roll but have been frequent attendants at Potomac Grange meetings to participate in assigned programs. Governmental problems under consideration are often referred to Potomac Grange committees for intensive study and discussion. Conclusions and recommendations are reported to the National Grange and have proved of enormous value in the shaping of Grange policies. Top government and organization people in Washington on special committees of Potomac Grange have given generously of their time in helping to make studies to form Grange policies.

In November, 1965, at the 99th annual session of the National Grange at Topeka, Kans., delegates voted to request that Potomac Grange No. 1 make two timely studies: whether it is feasible that a percentage of Federal Income Tax receipts be returned to the states; and a further study of the desirability of the U.S. returning to the gold standard and/or redeemable currency.

Examples of other recent important studies undertaken by Potomac Grange are:

Pros and Cons of Fluoridation of Public Water Supplies
Wage and Hour Legislation and the Farmer
Payments in Lieu of Taxes to State and Local Governments Containing Large Public Land Holdings
Report on Percentage Depletion as It Applies to Petroleum and Other Extractive Industries
Advantages and Disadvantages of Applying Minimum Wage Laws to Agricultural Workers
Coordinated Noxious Weed Control
Child Labor
Are We Growing Sufficient Sawtimber for National Requirements?
Exercise of the Powers of Eminent Domain
Federal Ownership of Oil and Mineral Rights in the States
Improvement in Agricultural Foreign Trade Relations
Uniform Traffic Laws and Ordinances
Reasons for Delay in Extending Adequate Telephone Service to American Farms
Uses of Atomic Energy in Agriculture
Financing of a National Highway Program
Controlling Water Pollution
Land Classification as a Guide in Production Adjustment Programs

HOME of Fredonia Grange, No. 1, in Chautauqua County, New York, first actual working Subordinate Grange unit.

Fredonia No. 1

The first genuine Grange which "lived, breathed, and had a being" was organized in Fredonia, N.Y. by Founder Oliver Hudson Kelley himself. This was the first and only permanent unit he succeeded in starting on his first memorable trip of organizing Granges from Washington, D. C. to his home near Itasca Landing, Minn., in the spring of 1868.

Today, in Fredonia, the conspicuous Grange Hall on the main street of the community continues to stand out with its front lettered windows on a white background and the words "Fredonia Grange No. 1." A large tablet says, "Organized April 16, 1868. Erected 1915."

Elizabeth L. Crocker, in a most interesting essay in her weekly column "Yesterdays" in *The Fredonia Censor* (published also in book form), tells the dramatic story of how Fredonia Grange No. 1 started. Here are some excerpts:

> Mr. Kelley resigned his position in the Department of Agriculture in February, 1868, to devote his entire time in an effort to organize Granges. He worked alone and under great hardships including limited finances. An invitation from Mr. A. S. Moss of Fredonia, with whom he had become acquainted previously and who was at the time assistant steward in the National Grange, brought him here. With the assistance of Mr. Moss, Mr. Kelley formed here the first regularly organized Grange in the world. This was the real foundation of the Order with members paying initiation fees and dues.
>
> It was in Armory Hall in the Woleben Block, nearly opposite the present Grange Hall, that Mr. Kelley met with a few of the leading citizens of Fredonia for the purpose of organizing.
>
> On December 16, 1868 the ladies were admitted for the first time when 21 were initiated.
>
> People engaged in pursuits other than that of agriculture became interested in Grange No. 1 here in Fredonia and many joined the organization. Had the attendance at the Grange meetings depended entirely upon the members living in the rural areas the Order might not have been able to survive.
>
> The section was sparsely settled, the roads were poor, the traveling slow and the farmers were very busy clearing and cultivating their lands. Therefore, it was not easy for them to get to the meetings.

Miss Crocker goes on to tell how the Grange members secured a lot for $2,000 on which to build their building and then they raised funds through entertainment and sales of $5400 with which to start. They financed the complete building cost of $13,000 through issuing certificates of indebtedness paying 5 percent interest which were oversubscribed by members.

Miss Crocker ended her column about Fredonia Grange by this general statement:

> The Grange has accomplished a great deal in the effort to make life more comfortable and more secure for all. It exerted great influence in securing rural free delivery of mail and of parcel post and its influence has been felt in the regulation of public utilities, the establishment of experiment stations, in conservation and forestry, farm credit and better highways. The members have been able to cooperate in purchasing farm supplies. One of the most important accomplishments was the establishment of various kinds of insurance. The members are always on the alert for state and national legislation that will tend to benefit all people. The interest and efforts of the members are ever evident in all social, educational and economic fields.

Green Mountain No. 1

The first subordinate Grange organized in the entire New England area, and this also by Founder Kelley, was at St. Johnsbury, Vt., on July 4, 1871.

It has been described in the last few years as the "Gibraltar" of the Grange because of its influence on the development of the Grange idea in the New England area of the United States. Its activities have long been an inspiration to other Granges in Vermont and in nearby states.

EXAMPLE OF PIONEER GRANGE — Minnehaha Grange No. 398, Edina, Minn., home state of Grange Founder Oliver H. Kelley, whose portrait hangs in its hall, was chartered in 1873 and has been active ever since. It is but an example of the far-flung, long-time influence the Grange has had in many parts of the country.

9

Grange Ritualism — Development, Meaning

While the Grange does not live for or by Ritual alone, the Ritualistic structure is the lifeblood of the Order. It is the ingredient that brings us together in harmonious relationship to work for the good of all people everywhere.

The teachings of the ritual enable our Order to be political without being partisan, religious without being denominational, and though it binds its members with a strong fraternal tie, it assures a complete individuality.

—C. Jerome Davis
Field Assistant to
the National Master

To the Grange ritual—its beauty, its moral and spiritual influence, its patriotism and idealism—is attributed much of the deep feeling that members today have for the Order. Through this ritual since its beginning, the Grange has built and developed the best in men and women, bringing out the finer side of life and elevating the thoughts and practices of each member.

It is beautifully said in the Preamble to the Constitution of the National Grange, that:

. . . Unity of action cannot be acquired without discipline, and discipline cannot be enforced without significant organization; hence, we have a ceremony of initiation which binds us in mutual fraternity as with a band of iron; but, although its influence is so powerful, its application is as gentle as that of the silken thread that binds a wreath of flowers.

Underlying the material accomplishments of which the Founders dreamed for the Grange in their plans to serve the needs of rural people in every possible way, they prepared a fraternal ritual based upon the most exalted views of God and nature. The symbols come from nature and the art of farming. This plan was in the first recorded statement on the Grange in a letter written by Founder Oliver H. Kelley to Founder William Saunders in August, 1867. Kelley said:

I suggest the project of organizing an Order to embrace in its membership those persons interested in cultivating the soil. I should make it a secret order, with several degrees, and signs and pass words. The lectures in each degree should be practical, appertaining to agricultural work, and at the same time convey a moral lesson. While the Order would aim to advance agriculture to a higher rank, by encouraging education, it would at the same time naturally em-

Grange Ritualism

First Degree	Faith	Spring	Laborer	Maid
Second Degree	Hope	Summer	Cultivator	Shepherdess
Third Degree	Charity	Autumn	Harvester	Gleaner
Fourth Degree	Fidelity	Winter	Husbandman	Matron

The higher degrees, Fifth, Sixth, and Seventh, are degrees of Pomona, Flora, and Ceres or Demeter and are conferred by Pomona Granges which are normally county Granges or District Granges depending upon the state; by the State Granges for the degree of Flora; by the National Grange in annual session of the Assembly of Demeter, in the case of the degree of Ceres.

These degrees are available to all those who fully subscribe to the long-established custom of teaching by symbols and emblems, to the principle of using the power of ritualism to bring out the finer characteristics of the members and the beauty of rural life.

brace the benefits to its members guaranteed by Masonry. Every tool used by farmers and gardeners could be emblems of the Order in some degree, and each could convey a practical and moral lesson.

About a month later in a letter to Anson Bartlett, of Ohio, he made this further statement:

Country and town societies and clubs are interesting for awhile, but soon lose their interest, and I see nothing that will be lasting, unless it combines with it the advantages which an Order similar to our Masonic Fraternity will provide. Among the objects in view may be mentioned a cordial and social fraternity of the farmers all over the country. Encourage them to read and think; to plant fruits and flowers, beautify their homes; elevate them; make them progressive. In our lectures in the various degrees, just see what a fund of beautiful material we have to make them sublime. Every tool the farmer works with, and all his surroundings, the beauties of nature, can convey a moral illustrated lesson, and in the labors of the farm also,—the preparation of the soil (the mind) for the seed (ideas)—planting—the harvest, etc.

While in Masonry there is much that is speculative, there will be in this Order little else but operative features. It will not call the members' minds from their work, but every tool they touch upon the farm in their daily labors, will call up some good thing they have learned in the Lodge.

Effective and Constructive Tie that Binds

Thus, during these first 100 years of the Grange its ritualism has been the effective and constructive tie that has bound together those who recognize the Brotherhood of Man as the finest expression of the Fatherhood of God.

The unusually fitting ritualism of the Grange, as reflected in the everyday experience of the farmer, is a constant reminder of man's actual partnership with the Almighty in producing a harvest of food and fiber.

Prominently featured is the Grange Cornucopia—the Horn of Plenty. This symbol is interpreted as teaching the lesson that we are *to dispense* as well as *to accumulate;* not to gather simply for the sake of possession but through proper use of our plenty, be prepared to share our abundance with others not so fortunate.

Another important feature about the value of the Ritualism in binding members together is the fact that the Grange member in Maine finds the Grange door in Oregon opening as readily to his signal as in his own Grange 3,000 miles away. Were it not for this universal tie, a national organization might soon deteriorate into state or local groups and its strong cohesive power be broken as indeed happened to approximately 500 other national farm and rural organizations which did not have this cohesive fraternal tie, even though it is conceded that there may have been many other factors in their demise.

Throughout Grange history the ritual has dramatized the beauty and importance of the family, home, community, and agriculture. Grange ritual is a vital part of regular procedure, meetings, and activities.

Early discussions by the Founders on the Ritualism and its formulation indicated an almost uncanny "premonition" of what was correct, solid, and appealing. Their thinking and their actions were remarkable in effectiveness and completeness. Their work has stood the test of 100 years and now goes forward into its second century with experience, stature, breadth of organizational structure, and with a firm foundation upon which to build an even more significant Grange in rural, suburban, and agricultural America.

How the Grange Was Designed

First thought of the Founders was to divide the work into three degrees as is done in the Masonic Order. It was soon realized that the four seasons of the year would form a more appropriate basis for Grange ritual.

Most fraternal orders feature lessons from the Bible as a part of the ritual, and the same thing was to be done in this new fraternity. In many orders Faith, Hope, and Charity, are used as the principal lessons of the degrees, and it was evidently intended from the beginning to use these three Christian Graces as the foundation lessons. When it was decided to have four degrees, it became necessary to select a fourth lesson that would be a fit companion to these three. The lesson finally chosen was "Fidelity"—one of the most important attributes of civilized man.

It would be impossible to select four words more full of meaning than Faith, Hope, Charity, and Fidelity, or four virtues of more significance than these in our Christian civilization—or in rural life.

There are at least 43 direct quotations from the Bible in the ritual of the first four degrees, besides many indirect quotations, and allusions to matters contained in the Bible.

OUTSTANDING Youth Degree Team, exemplifying the Third Degree of the 92nd Annual Session of the Oregon State Grange, June 1965. Excellence in Grange Degree work has long proven to be the recipe for permanence in Grange interest and activity on the part of young people.

Ritual Stations Based on Old English Estate

Careful study of the ritual reveals that those who planned it had in mind the old-time large English estate which was a quite complete world in itself, and lends itself to ritualistic purposes much better than would the American type of farm estate. The Grange Master's desk represents the mansion, (or baronial castle) of the estate set in its own park-like enclosure, and approached through a broad avenue of trees. Another part of the estate was the farm or "grange" with its many little fields, usually fenced with hedges, and with the people who actually tilled the land living in the small farm village.

Grange officers are similar to the officers of this old baronial estate. The entrance to the estate, for instance, was closed by a massive gate, which was opened and closed by the *Gate Keeper,* who, with his family, lived in the gate keeper's lodge located beside the entrance. In the earlier days when might alone was right, his function in guarding the gate was an extremely important one. The owl is used as the emblem of the gate keeper because its habit of being awake at night makes it a fitting emblem for a watchman, which was the function of the gate keeper.

The *Overseer* had the duties that his name implies, and in addition to the supervision of the farming operations, (or the husbandry as it was called) often also had charge of the upkeep of the park-like grounds surrounding the mansion.

The *Lecturer,* while not an officer of the English estate, never-the-less was included as an important station in the basic design of the Grange. His contributions are extremely vital throughout Grange organization and activities. (See also p. 72.)

The *Steward* was in a way the executive secretary of the estate. He made most of the purchases. He also had charge of the tools and supplies of the grange, and was the business agent of the whole enterprise.

To a large measure the physical comfort of those living on the estate was dependent upon his efficiency.

Even the *Chaplain* was in an official position, and his living, so-called, was provided by the estate, in which was located the little church, the entire expense of which was paid by the master's income, and not by the subscriptions of the congregation.

The Grange Hall, therefore, is meant to typify in miniature this farm estate with its palace, and park, and Grange or farm proper.

Women Early Had Important Roles in Grange

The Grange was the first fraternal organization to make the wise move of admitting women to membership upon full equality with the men. So, when it was decided to invite the women to join it seemed desirable to create certain offices for them. The need of a Lady *Assistant Steward,* for instance, was obvious, and in addition the Founders called upon Roman mythology for the names of three women officers, selected from the goddesses whose functions were the protection of growing things, though the ritualism itself is based on Greek mythology—and indeed on the Eleusinian rites of 25 centuries ago into which only the outstanding citizens were eligible.

CERES was the goddess who presented to mankind the great gift of grain upon which we depend to such a large extent for our sustenance. She had care over the cereals which are named after her, and over the grower of the grains.

INSTALLATION CEREMONY—The Worthy High Priest of Demeter, E. Carroll Bean (back to camera) installing National Ceres, Pomona, and Flora (Mrs. C. Jerome Davis of Indiana, Mrs. Edgar Hall of West Virginia, and Mrs. Bernice Knight of Texas, r to l in the center of the picture); at the 99th Annual Session of the National Grange, in Topeka, Kan. This same installation ceremony is used some 6000 times each year in installing officers of Subordinate, Pomona, and State Granges.

Others are Mrs. Forrest Mowry of Rhode Island, Emblem Bearer (extreme left); Mrs. Arthur Perkins of Maine, Lady Marshal (at the left of Mrs. Davis or over the High Priest's shoulder); Mrs. Allen McComb of Tennessee, Regalia Bearer (at the extreme right).

POMONA was the goddess who presided over fruits, and to whom the fruit growers appealed for protection of their products and for an abundant yield.

FLORA was the goddess of flowers and of Spring, and to her was due the fact that the earth is so beautifully adorned with flowers.

More than equality has been given women, as it will be seen, for while a woman can hold any office in the Grange, there are four of the offices that are not open to men.

Lessons from the Bible

The terminology of farming as adopted by the Grange in its ritual is so very appropriate in illustrating lessons of the Bible. Practically all the words of Christ were spoken in the open. He drew largely upon agriculture for His similes and illustrations. Among the 43 or more direct quotations from the Bible, as mentioned earlier in this text, the Subordinate Grange ritualism embraces the following significant applications:

"The shepherd goeth before the sheep," He said and in many other instances used the shepherd and the sheep to designate Himself and His followers.

Note also the parable of the seed, "Some fell by the wayside and the fowls came and devoured them up. Some fell upon stony places and the sun scorched them. Some fell among thorns and the thorns choked them. But some fell into good soil and brought forth fruit, some an hundred-fold, some sixty-fold, some thirty-fold."

The vine and the vineyard are often used as similes in both the Old and the New Testament.

The psalmist said, "I will lift up mine eyes unto the hills whence cometh my help."

And again He said, "He causeth the grass to grow for the cattle, and herb for the service of man."

Well-conducted ritualistic work is a matter of prime importance in the Grange. It is an outlet for the dramatic ability of members and a degree team that works conscientiously can find full scope for the display of all of its dramatic genius. Moreover, it can find in the degree work the same enjoyment that is found in the presentation of plays and dramas. As a matter of fact, Grange ritualism permits thousands of patrons to participate in its attractive features, thus developing their interest in the Order, and at the same time building their own proper attitude toward improving their fellowmen and the world in which we live.

Structure of Grange Ritualism

It will be seen from the chart on page 44 that the first four degrees are conferred by the Subordinate Grange and the Fifth Degree is conferred by the county or Pomona Grange. Its beautifully constructed Fifth Degree lessons are designed to be a fitting next step after the Four Degrees of the Subordinate Granges.

This impressive Fifth Degree has been greatly perfected in recent years with the degree and drill teams providing an impressive, long-remembered, inspiring stage setting and words of wisdom.

The Sixth Degree is now conferred exclusively by State Masters as a beautiful Floral court scene over which Worthy Flora, Goddess of Flowers, presides. There seems to be no limit to what State Granges have done in presenting the ritual through beautiful and inspiring mystic stage decorations, rose drills and other appropriate features and spectacles.

Jurisdiction over the ritualism of the First to the Sixth Degree is vested in the National Master of the Grange, as well as final determination on all matters of law and order and of the manuals of the Junior Granges, Subordinate Granges, Pomona Granges and State Granges and all of their degree work.

From the very beginning, the Seventh Degree was envisioned as the highest or climax degree. This degree would not only interpret all of the ritualism of the Subordinate, Pomona, and State Granges, but it would be drawn from the most spectacular agriculture ritual in all the world's history.

Extensive research then was being done by the Greek Archaeological Society near the little town of Elevsis, some 18 miles northwest of Athens, Greece.

Founder Francis M. McDowell, who is credited for linking agriculture with the mythical teachings of earlier centuries in the Seventh Degree, was elected (in 1868) the first High Priest of the Assembly of Demeter, the controlling body of Ritualism of the Seventh Degree.

The first time this beautiful Seventh Degree was conferred was in Nashville, Tennessee, at the 18th Annual Session of the National Grange in 1884 on eight candidates. Over the years since then conferring of the Seventh Degree has become one of the outstanding events of Grange

NEW BEAUTIFUL SEVENTH DEGREE OF CERES Certificate presented to those who attain this high Grange honor. The memorable illustration is of the original temple of Ceres.

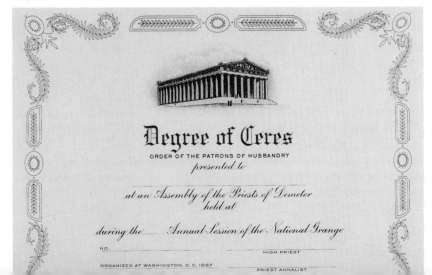

Degree of Ceres

ORDER OF THE PATRONS OF HUSBANDRY

presented to

at an Assembly of the Priests of Demeter
held at

during the   Annual Session of the National Grange

NO.

HIGH PRIEST

ORGANIZED AT WASHINGTON, D. C. 1867

PRIEST ANNALIST

Annual Sessions, with nearly a quarter of a million members having received this degree so far.

Assembly of Demeter

All Grangers who have had the Seventh Degree conferred on them and who retain good standing in a Subordinate Grange become members of the Assembly of Demeter.

The Assembly of Demeter is also the custodian of the secret or unwritten work, the signs, the patrons' test, etc., and it is from the High Priest of the Assembly of Demeter that the annual passwords emanate. The High Priest has the responsibility for determining all matters relating to the secret work, and in relation to the Seventh Degree between Annual Sessions.

He personally originates the annual passwords—Subordinate, Pomona, and Junior—and communicates them to the Master of the National Grange in connection with the conferring of the Seventh Degree.

The Assembly of Demeter holds three sessions a year: the session at which the Seventh Degree is conferred; the annual ritualistic convocation, at which secret work is demonstrated and reviewed; and a business convocation to transact routine business and discuss any matters resulting from action of the National Grange. Assembly of Demeter officers are elected biennially at this session.

The Assembly of Demeter is also the "Supreme Court" of the Grange and may serve, if ever necessary, as a Court of final appeal in which charges against officers of the National Grange can be preferred.

Non-Farm Rural Families as Grange Members

Recalling Founder Kelley's original thoughts in his letter of August, 1867, to Anson Bartlett (page 44), Grange ritual *has been* largely based on "operative features" with emphasis on the agricultural implements and the symbols of man's daily labors in partnership with the Almighty in producing food and fiber.

The "speculative" elements of the Grange ritual—the beauty and significance of its inspiring and stimulating gospel of man's relationship to Divine Nature—are there, but *have been* glowing only in the background.

Now, in America, since rural and suburban non-farm people are the fastest-growing segment of our population in most states, it would seem that the second century of the Grange could well take account of this shift in emphasis from the purely rural.

The Grange has been unique for 100 years as a rural family fraternity. But, is it not possible that rural and suburban non-farm families can also be exhorted to avail themselves, to their everlasting benefit, of the matchless beauty and intriguing "lessons" in the Grange's beautiful agricultural ritual?

10

Recognition Given Grange Policies, Objectives, National Position

Over the years, as the Grange grew in prestige, stature, and practical help to farm families, it became the recipient of glowing commendations.

The members, in their own way, commend their Grange Subordinate, Pomona, state, and national officers for outstanding accomplishments, but from the outside—from national and international leaders—have come messages of deep interest in its activities, and appreciation indicating how the Grange has lived up to its birthright.

Only a few of these heartfelt statements can be included here—it would take a publication as big as this to quote them all. For example, every President of the United States from Ulysses S. Grant to Lyndon B. Johnson has been friendly to the Grange and each, in strong public statements, has endorsed Grange activities, ideals, and contributions to the American way of life and progress. Two Presidents have attended Annual Sessions of the Grange. Since the very beginning, the White House has continuously encouraged Grange officers and members in their efforts to bring about better conditions for farmers and their communities.

LYNDON B. JOHNSON

"I have always had the highest regard and respect for your great organization. I have many dear and close friends in the National Grange—including your Master, Herschel Newsom. For many years—in Congress and the Senate, and now as President—I have valued his counsel. I have never found it to be other than wise, thoughtful and responsible. Yours is a record and a history that are rich and constructive.

"The National Grange has been a unifying force in rural America for nearly a century. It has sought to educate farmers and non-farmers alike on the need for a strong farm family, agriculture and a prosperous and stable rural America. Yet, while you have been the advocate of the nation's farm families, the National Grange has never demanded for farmers that which was not also in the public interest.

"Your leadership in rural America has never been more indispensable than it is today. The one-third of our people who live in rural America must be full participants in the great society that together we shall build. We seek parity of income for farmers, and we shall seek this goal within the framework of commodity programs designed to strengthen and improve farm income. As part of the effort to improve the incomes of farmers, we shall seek particularly to continue to strengthen markets abroad for U.S. food and fiber. . . ."

JOHN F. KENNEDY

"The thousands of Grange halls which dot the nation, all of them community centers for civil, spiritual and social activities, continuously enrich our open society. The counsel of Grange leaders, and the cooperation and understanding of member families, are vital to the operation of national farm programs dedicated to strengthening the family farm system under which our agriculture has become the most productive of all time.

"Through the 95 years of your organization's history, Grangers have been concerned with the responsibilities of total citizenship as well as the problems and the progress of agriculture. I am confident this philosophy will prevail in the challenging and promising days ahead."

DWIGHT D. EISENHOWER

"A critical test for any organization is the challenge of a national emergency and the demand made on its members for quick and full service to the country. This is a test which the National Grange has met with distinction. In times of peace, also, it has proved a vital force for the welfare of agriculture and the Nation. The Grange, through the years, has earned the respect and appreciation of America."

HARRY S. TRUMAN

"Who more than a boy who grew up on a farm and who was afterwards an active farmer realizes the value of the work of the National Grange? Its contributions to the American farmer and to farm life generally have been beyond measure. I am proud of my membership in so constructive a body."

FRANKLIN D. ROOSEVELT

"For many years I have been a member of the Grange. I have felt at home in it because it embodies the fine flavor of rural living which I myself have known and loved. Beyond this, it has been an instrument for expressing in useful activity the highest sentiments and deepest loyalties of Americans."

PRESIDENT EISEN-HOWER DEDICATES NEW NATIONAL GRANGE HEADQUARTERS — The President shown in front of the building with National Master Herschel Newsom.

SENATORS AT 99TH ANNUAL GRANGE SESSION, TOPEKA—Senator Everett Dirksen (Ill.) speaking, with Senators Frank Carlson (Kan.) and Carl E. Mundt (Kan.) at head table. Both the Senators Carlson and Mundt are long-time Grange members, and all have had distinguished records of service in public affairs. Senator Dirksen has said about the Grange: "The National Grange, with its self-governing subordinate units, is typically American. The high standards set and stressed have not only bene-fited its own members but also have contributed to the welfare of the Nation—yes, even the entire World."

HERBERT HOOVER

"The Grange not only aids in realizing the conception of a rich and rounded rural life, but helps to build into our national fibre the ideals of sound citizenship and patriotic service. It is clearly one of the most salutary forces in American Life."

CALVIN COOLIDGE

"The progressive conservatism of the Grange and its sensible way of considering farm problems and presenting farm needs has given it a position of influence in the Nation and has led those in positions of responsibility to listen to the views of the Grange with consideration and respect."

HUBERT H. HUMPHREY

"The spirit of fraternity and cooperation which is so much a part of the philosophy of the Grange makes this organization more than an economic institution. Actually, the Grange represents the social, spiritual, and economic aspects of rural life. It has been and continues to be a constructive and valuable force in the life of this nation."

ORVILLE L. FREEMAN

"The Grange's traditional objectives . . . character building, encouragement of education, promotion of sound legislation, and the ready acceptance of individual and community responsibility . . . are known and appreciated by all who are working for the betterment of agriculture and the social, cultural and economic development of rural America.

"The Grange's active support of America's efforts to solve the world food crisis without jeopardizing the domestic farm economy lends new dimensions, greater stature and more significance to that organization.

"American agriculture's importance in achieving international peace and cooperation cannot be minimized, for to achieve those goals the levels of nutrition and the standards of living must be elevated for all the peoples of the world.

"The thrust the National Grange is helping to give this all-important effort is both recognized and welcomed by the Secretary of Agriculture, and now, as the Grange nears its 100th Annual Session, I offer my enthusiastic congratulations and best wishes."

JOHN EDGAR HOOVER

"The National Grange is part of our American heritage of freedom, initiative and courage. You have fought valiantly for those principles which have made America great. You stand as a beacon of strength, working not alone for the America of today but also the America of tomorrow.

"The principles exemplified by the National Grange are today greatly needed by America. The increasing lawlessness, civil disobedience and extremism, both of the left and right, are weakening our Nation. Vigilantism, draft card burnings, anihilist disrespect for law and order, seriously injure our cause. We need an increased awareness of our responsibilities as citizens. Each person in a free society must be willing to do his share.

"We in the FBI appreciate the steadfast cooperation of the National Grange. Only in this cooperative endeavor can we keep our country free."

ELEANOR ROOSEVELT

"I think the Granges are very useful to the rural communities and have contributed a great deal to rural life."

(Editor's Note: *"As Others See Us"* is an excellent booklet compiled in 1962 by the Washington County Pomona Grange No. 58 of the State of Indiana and dedicated to National Master Herschel D. Newsom and Blanche Newsom, which has scores of quotations from national and local leaders about the Grange.)

GRANGE WEEK

Year after year, governors throughout the country proclaim a given week as "Grange Week," urging citizens of all communities to cooperate in its observance. This quotation from a Proclamation by Governor Nelson A. Rockefeller, of New York, is typical of the sentiments and language used by leading governors in calling attention to the prestige, public appreciation, and service today of Subordinate, Pomona, and State Granges:

"For almost a century the Grange, in New York and elsewhere, has been one of our most valued and valuable institutions.

"Some years ago its merits were described as follows: 'The Grange is a great farm fraternity: building character; developing leadership; encouraging education; promoting community betterment; instilling an appreciation of high ideals; teaching through work and play the value of co-operation and service in the attainment of happiness.'

"The definition still holds good. In the Empire State the Grange has been a vital force in legislation, promoting laws for the protection of the interests of those engaged in agriculture, as well as others.

"The organization has also rendered admirable service by promoting neighborliness in rural neighborhoods. This in turn has made our whole State a closely knit community, with consequent benefits enhancing the prosperity and prestige of the State."

✧   ✧   ✧   ✧   ✧

In 1966, 35 Governors in Proclamations containing tributes to the ideals and program of the Grange asked public observance of Grange Week, April 17-23. Grange Week in 1967 will be April 16-22.

11

The 16 National Masters

As striking in favorable effect on the progress of the Grange as were the decisions and follow-through of the Founders, have been the inspired, active, far-sighted administrations of the 16 Masters of the National Grange during its first 100 years.

Today's Master, Herschel D. Newsom, exemplifies the ability, fervor, deep religious and practical attributes which are rare, but seem to be the rule among Grange Masters.

These brief biographical sketches of the Masters prove the point and *also* compliment the membership and other Grange officials for their good judgment in the process of selection.

16. Herschel D. Newsom 1950-

Sixteenth Master of the National Grange, Mr. Newsom, elected in 1950, comes from an Indiana family of farmers for five generations. Mr. and Mrs. Newsom continue to maintain their farm home near Columbus, Indiana, in addition to their Washington residence. They have two sons, Jesse Richard and David H.

Mr. Newsom received his A.B. degree in Chemistry from Indiana University in 1926, and the University's Distinguished Alumni Award in 1960.

Like his ancestors, he is a member of the Society of Friends. He represents the third generation in the Newsom family to take an active part in Grange affairs, having first been elected Gatekeeper of his Juvenile (now Junior) Grange, as well as in public affairs, generally, especially as they influence rural life.

In 1963, he became the eighth president of the International Federation of Agricultural Producers, a federation of farm organizations from five continents founded in London in 1946, and was reelected in 1964. He is also Chairman of the Committee on World Food Crisis.

He is a member of the U. S. Food for Peace Council; Trustee of the American Freedom from Hunger Foundation; Director, United Nations Association of the U. S. A.; member, Transportation Council of the De-

LEADING THE NATION AND THE WORLD—National Master Herschel D. Newsom delivers the IFAP address at the UN Food and Agriculture Organization meeting in Rome, Italy. The farm leader served 1963-66 as president of the International Federation of Agricultural Producers, is chairman of the World Food Crisis Committee, trustee of the American Freedom from Hunger Foundation and takes part in many other international groups.

partment of Commerce; Trustee, Joint Council on Economic Education; a charter member of the Advisory Council of the International Movement for Atlantic Union, Inc.; and member, Inter-American Economic Policy Committee on Canadian-American Relations and Advisory Committee on Latin-American Relations.

He holds the following Presidential appointments: President's Advisory Committee on Trade Negotiations, Citizen's Commission on International Cooperation, President's Commission on the Employment of the Handicapped, President's Rural Safety Council, and Citizen's Committee for International Development. Mr. Newsom held similar appointments from President Truman, President Eisenhower, and President Kennedy.

He is also a member of the Advisory Committee on Agricultural Cooperatives to the Agency for International Development and some 25 other foundations, committees and boards, including the National Livestock and Meat Board, Foundation for American Agriculture, Agricultural Committee of the National Planning Association, the Farm Film Foundation, National Highway Users Conference, Committee on Rural Scouting, Boy Scouts of America, CARE, Agricultural Hall of Fame, American Institute of Cooperation, and Credit Union National Association.

He is a Director and Vice President of the Farmers and Traders Life Insurance Company, Syracuse, N. Y., and Director of the National Grange Mutual Insurance Company of Keene, N. H.

15. Henry D. Sherwood 1950

Master of the New York State Grange, and Overseer of the National Grange, Henry D. Sherwood was installed as National Master to fill the gap caused by the untimely death October 25, 1950 of National Master Albert S. Goss. Mr. Sherwood became National Master on the next day, and served until the installation of Herschel D. Newsom in November, 1950.

14. Albert S. Goss 1941-1950

Born in Rochester, N. Y., Mr. Goss was educated on the West Coast and as a young man engaged in milling and farming. For a time he conducted a telephone business and a country store.

His Grange career covered some 35 years beginning with the Finley Grange No. 414 in Washington. Its cooperative activities intrigued him and in 1920 he was made manager of the Grange Cooperative Wholesale, Seattle, and was then elected State Master, in 1922.

He experienced a steady rise in Grange leadership and attracted wide attention for his work to improve policies of the Federal Farm Loan Board. His prominence in land bank activities resulted in President Franklin D. Roosevelt naming him Land Bank Commissioner in the dark days of 1933.

ANNUALLY for many years the National Grange Office has entertained the newly-elected National Officers of Future Farmers of America. Here Past Master Albert S. Goss, is in conference with the 1948 National Officers of FFA, at Grange Headquarters then at 744 Jackson Place, Washington, D. C. In addition to the FFA National Officers, the National Advisor, Bill Spanton (at extreme left) along with other advisors and counsellors of FFA.

He will always be greatly remembered by thousands of farmers who found him a friend indeed when they were in financial distress. He resigned as Land Bank Commissioner on June 16, 1940 preceding his election as National Master in November, 1941.

Recognized as one of the keenest students of economics and finance, he was an authority in the Federal Land Bank field and also helped to formulate a program of cooperative production credit which later became the model for the Farm Credit Administration. During World War II, he was prominently identified with numerous war activities and was often called in for consultation by the White House and government department heads. He was active also in helping to solve world agricultural problems, and assisted in the organization of the International Federation of Agricultural Producers.

13. Louis J. Taber 1923-1941

The second Ohio man to become National Master, Louis J. Taber of Mount Pleasant, Ohio, learned the underlying principles of a successful life in the "school of hard knocks" when he was 14 years old. The death of his father threw on his shoulders the full management of the family farm.

He became active in organizing Belmont Grange No. 889 at Barnesville, Ohio, and rose through the stations to State Master. He resigned to become State Director of Agriculture in 1921.

PAST NATIONAL MASTER TABER'S LAST MEETING—Standing (right) is Louis J. Taber, Past Master of the National Grange (1923-1941) as he presided for the last time as Chairman of the Board of Directors of the Farmers and Traders Life Insurance Company. Standing with Mr. Taber is Edwin E. Henne, then President of the Company. At extreme left is Alvin E. Hanson, late President of the Insurance Company, who made the initial arrangements for publishing this book as well as for creating the Grange Meditation Center at the National Soldier's Cemetery at Gettysburg.

His outstanding Grange and public work resulted in his elevation to National Master in 1923. He was a dynamic, forceful speaker who inspired his audiences.

Mr. Taber was honored by the Juvenile Granges of the nation in 1941 by creation of a living forest known as the "Louis J. Taber Forest" in Wayne National Forest in Hocking County, Southeastern Ohio. A memorial park was also dedicated at Barnesville, Ohio, July 5, 1947 as another appreciation for services rendered to agriculture and rural life by Mr. Taber.

Following his retirement from the position of Master of the National Grange, Mr. Taber became president of the Farmers and Traders Life Insurance Company (a company organized as a result of action of the delegate body of the National Grange). He served as its president during a decade when the original plan was in jeopardy to mutualize this life insurance company which could only be organized under New York laws as a stock company originally. The mutualization was advanced very substantially during the period of time when Mr. Taber served as president.

12. Sherman J. Lowell 1919-1923

A rugged personality, vigorous and aggressive, characterized Mr. Lowell of Fredonia, N. Y., site of Fredonia Grange No. 1, first and oldest Subordinate in the U. S. He became an extensive fruit farmer and grape grower in the famed Chautauqua County vineyard area, being identified with various agricultural groups, and active in local banking circles. For 10 years he was manager of the Pomfret Fruit Company, largest fruit shipping concern at Fredonia.

After joining Fredonia Grange No. 1, he moved steadily through all the Subordinate, Pomana, and State Grange offices, serving as State Master until his elevation to National Master in November, 1919. After the death of Oliver Wilson, the 11th Master, in 1924, Mr. Lowell was elected Archon of the Assembly of Demeter, holding that position until 1929.

11. Oliver Wilson 1911-1919

Master for eight years after a hotly contested election campaign, the administration of Oliver Wilson, of Illinois, was a period noteworthy for complete unity and many advances. A record 3339 new Granges were established during his term of office. And, for the first time, Grange approval was given to equal suffrage for women by constitutional amendment. Federal aid for highway improvement was increasingly advocated; and endorsement was given to prohibition, to pure food legislation, and to better protection of national resources.

Mr. Wilson strongly emphasized the desirability of more recognition for farm women and greater emphasis on Home Economics work in the Grange.

It was during his administration that the Golden Jubilee was celebrated with National Master Oliver Wilson presiding, and President Woodrow Wilson giving an able address on the opening day of the National Session held at Washington, D. C., in November, 1916.

10. Nahum J. Bachelder 1905-1911

Bringing to the Master's position not only a long experience in Grange leadership, including six years as National Lecturer, Mr. Bachelder also brought a wide knowledge of public affairs. His service as a former governor of New Hampshire greatly enhanced the prestige of position of the National Master. This legislative background aided his standing as a spokesman for the American farmer and rural families.

Among public projects given impetus were the establishment of independent cooperative enterprises, particularly cooperative elevators, building and loan associations, warehouses, and Grange fire insurance. His attitude was that such enterprises, instead of being owned and administered directly by the National Grange, were best operated as individual agencies, but with the backing and active support of the Grange.

It was during Mr. Bachelder's administration that President Theodore Roosevelt's Country Life Commission was organized, and the Grange was commended for its assistance in arousing widespread interest throughout the country in the Commission and its purposes.

9. Aaron Jones 1897-1905

A man of tremendous energy, great vigor, and a thorough believer in farm organization, Aaron Jones, of Indiana, as an extensive farmer, realized the handicaps under which fellow farmers were forced to operate, as well as many injustices from which they were suffering.

His vigorous administration of eight years threw the full force of the Grange organization into the fight for farm equality. Among other accomplishments, he established good relations between the National Grange and the Federal Department of Agriculture.

The teaching of agriculture in the public schools, of which the Grange had been the first advocate, was given a decided boost by National Master Jones' insistence that such a subject be included in the curriculum.

Among practical legislative policies the Grange advocated in his time were those in favor of an effective parcel post system; against free railroad passes; favoring a standardized galvanized fence wire; and denouncing Congressional free seed distribution. Over several years Grange representatives fought for Congressional removal of the revenue tax from alcohol rendered unfit for beverage use. The result of this successful Grange agitation was to open up a substantial industry for the production of denatured alcohol—a cheap and safe fuel for light, power, and heat.

8. Joseph H. Brigham 1888-1897

Of forceful character and possessed of a fearlessness in action which stood him in good stead in this period of Grange history, Colonel Brigham, of Ohio, guided the Order in the midst of widespread agitation and many complications. Various national farm movements began to show themselves and Colonel Brigham's efforts kept the Grange "right side up."

Pure food legislation was claiming increasing interest, with the Grange taking a strong stand against adulteration and mislabeling. The long continued Grange agitation for rural mail delivery was bearing fruit and resulted in the establishment of R.F.D. routes in many states in 1896.

At the 25th anniversary observance in 1891 at Springfield, Ill., the Grange was reported to be apparently well headed on the upward climb of practical constructive service to agriculture. An anniversary proclamation was given wide publicity which urged universal support in behalf of further service to farm people.

7. James Draper 1888

On the untimely death in office of National Master Israel Putnam Darden, July 17, 1888, the Overseer of the National Grange, James Draper, Massachusetts State Master, stepped into the gap for the remaining months of 1888 until November, when Joseph H. Brigham was elected National Master.

6. Israel Putnam Darden 1885-1888

Identified with many civic movements in his own state of Mississippi, Mr. Darden was the second Southerner to be elected National Master.

He proved to be an earnest leader and helped the Grange weather a number of political situations which put the organization to a severe test. He challenged the members to become active in fighting for their rights. Even though the Grange was not to take a partisan position, the members and their organizations should accept their responsibility to work to protect their rights and interests. He urged Grangers, as responsible citizens, to use their ballots to send men to the legislatures and to Congress who would protect rather than exploit, farmers' interests.

5. Jonathan J. Woodman 1879-1885

Few Grange leaders ever faced a more serious task than did J. J. Woodman, of Michigan, when he took over the National Master's position in a period requiring reconstruction of Grange policies and operating procedures.

Mr. Woodman was a strong supporter of the educational program of the Grange, and he realized the farmer's need for progressive legislation affecting agriculture. He continued an energetic fight for an efficient Department of Agriculture with a seat in the President's Cabinet. He worked for laws to stop the spread of the contagious "cattle plague" which led to the establishment in 1895 of the Bureau of Animal Husbandry in the Department of Agriculture.

Under his wise management and during his third term, the Grange once more was on a sound financial and economic basis, and its prestige was growing.

4. Samuel E. Adams 1877-1879

Samuel E. Adams, of Minnesota, faced discouraging conditions, of which he was well aware, as he began his term as National Master. It was probably the low period of Grange history due to many national and other reasons that far-sighted and loyal Grange leaders were fighting to overcome. During his administration, a number of progressive programs were initiated, including the first recorded action by any group advocating the teaching of agriculture in public schools, and the first definite appointment of a Grange Legislative Committee to bring to the attention of Congress the recommendations of the Grange on legislative matters.

3. John T. Jones 1875-1877

It was during the administration of John Thompson Jones, of Arkansas, that the Grange was incorporated on April 6, 1876, in the State of Kentucky.

In the middle of National Master Jones' administration was the hectic Hayes-Tilden presidential controversy which developed widespread bitterness, the Grange demonstrating its inherent strength and importance as "the friend of the farmer."

Grange leaders were realizing that trouble and failure could follow if the principles established by the Founders 10 years previously were not followed. It was during this period of growing troubles that the Grange leaders of that day realized that the vision of the Founders for a real fraternity of the countryside, with high ideals and humanistic aims, should be the basis of their activities.

2. Dudley W. Adams 1873-1875

First Master of the Iowa State Grange, Dudley W. Adams was a man of broad vision equally enthusiastic with Founder Oliver Kelley over prospects for mighty results, but far more cautious than Kelley. He was the first Master of a State Grange to attend a national session in Washington, D.C., and in January, 1872, was elected National Master.

During his administration the new Grange movement was sweeping across the country like wild-fire. Farmers were rallying to the Grange banner by the thousands. National Master Adams was the first to see the need for caution in restricting the membership to legitimate farm and rural families. Speculators, demagogues, small politicians, grain buyers, cotton factors, and lawyers suddenly discovered they were "interested in agricultural pursuits" and besieged Grange officers to admit them to membership.

His words of caution are equally important today in that there be wise discrimination in the admission of new members. He warned: ". . . keep our gates closed against those whose interest is what they can make out of us. To have such admitted to our councils can only result in evil, and sow seeds of internal strife."

His efforts and those of Grange leaders around him were not entirely successful, and this led to serious problems a few years later that rocked the very foundations of the Grange organization.

It was also during the Adams' administration that the "Granger Laws" were progressing steadily toward enactment and the power of organized farmers was rapidly being revealed. (See Chapter 6.)

The comprehensive Grange *Declaration of Purposes* which so wisely defines the objectives of the Grange was developed under National Master Adams' guidance. It outlined a far-flung program designed to benefit producers and consumers alike, and set forth goals and objectives of such comprehensive worth that they have stood the test of time.

1. William Saunders 1867-1873

On the birthday of the Grange in William Saunders' office, on December 4, 1867, the seven Founders constituted themselves "The National Grange of the Patrons of Husbandry" and elected Mr. Saunders as the first National Master. A native of Scotland, he had come to America and had won outstanding recognition as a landscape architect. Three generations of his paternal ancestors had been prominent gardeners, and he followed in their footsteps.

At that time, he was Superintendent of the Propagating Gardens in the Department of Agriculture, with an office in a small brick building at the corner of Missouri Avenue and 4½ Street, Washington, D. C. This provided a convenient meeting place for the Founders. There they set up the Constitution, perfected the ritual, elected the first officers, prepared promotional material and visualized a great family fraternity of the countryside which lives now into its second century.

Excellent judgment and thoughtfulness guided his decisions as National Master, and he became an excellent balance wheel for the impulsive "Father" Kelley who was so often animated by emotion. His wide acquaintance and influence in agricultural and horticultural circles were helpful to the early organizational efforts of the Grange. Following his five years as National Master, he served on the executive committee for three years, continuing his valuable counsel.

III

What the Grange Stands for

The ultimate object of this organization is for mutual instruction and protection, to lighten labor by diffusing a knowledge of its aims and purposes, to expand the mind by tracing the beautiful laws the Great Creator has established in the Universe, and to enlarge our views of creative wisdom and power.

To those who read aright, history proves that in all ages society is fragmentary, and successful results of general welfare can be secured only by general effort. Unity of action cannot be acquired without discipline, and discipline cannot be enforced without significant organization; hence we have a ceremony of initiation which binds us in mutual fraternity as with a band of iron; but, although its influence is so powerful, its application is as gentle as that of the silken thread that binds a wreath of flowers.

—*From the Preamble to the*
CONSTITUTION OF THE NATIONAL GRANGE

YOUTH OFFICERS PRO-TEM AT THE NATIONAL GRANGE CONVENTION—
*Each year 22 young members from 22 different states wear the gold sash of the
National Offices and preside at one session of the National Grange Convention. Here
are the young people so honored at the 99th Annual Session of the National Grange
in 1965 (Topeka, Kansas).*

LEADERSHIP TRAINING STARTS EARLY—A young Kansas Granger assumes the role of Master at the 1965 National Grange Annual Session. The youth regularly "fill the chairs" of adult officers during a part of National Grange Sessions. In their own local meetings, the young people follow the same business procedure and hold the same offices as their adult counterparts.

12 What the Grange Stands for in

Personal Growth

True now, as it was 100 years ago, though we have more facilities today for education, for communication, for study, for travel, is the contribution the Grange makes to the *personal growth* of its members—men, women, boys, girls.

Right from the beginning, the Founders directed attention to the need for developing the Grange as an educational force. As a matter of fact, one of the original purposes was to *"advance the cause of education among ourselves and for our children by all just means within our power."*

How the Grange Helps the Individual

That the Grange helps the individual to grow in knowledge, ability, confidence, and leadership is widely known. For example, quoting a State Master:

So many of our best thinkers . . . the most progressive people in the community . . . are utterly incapable of expressing themselves in public on any ques-

67

tion, though vitally interested in it, or are lost when presiding at a meeting. Those who actually become active find that the Grange is a training school for these matters, and every Lecturer should be on the job, not neglecting one single opportunity to train the members along these lines.

A young married couple said:

> The Grange has given us many responsibilities and opportunities to advance in leadership. Just being a part of a committee gives one the chance to help make important decisions along with others that will give us practice in making decisions in our own lives. It has offered many opportunities to get up in front of groups and conduct meetings, talk, or even present programs. Many important happenings in our lives have been brought about by meeting Grangers who have given us advice and opportunities to better ourselves.

Early in Grange history, and quite true today in many parts of the country, is the fact that the Grange may be described as a "college" or "university" or "high school" for the grownups who did not have an opportunity as youths or children to attend such an educational institution.

Participation in Grange affairs, such as the give-and-take of discussion and debate in the forum for considering important, timely legislation and Grange policies and programs, has helped thousands of Grangers to grow and to develop latent powers. Through such participation, members acquire the ability to think, to speak, and to express their convictions. As a result, lives have become richer, fuller, more productive, more cultivated—often exalted.

The respect and high regard of fellow Grangers and other citizens in the community have surrounded these Grange members. Many have reached high positions of service and prestige in the Grange, in their community, state, nation, and the world.

PARADE OF THE STATES—The State Grange Princes and Princesses form a backdrop for the 1965 National Grange Prince and Princess. The Grange Youth Committee theme, "Every Second Counts" is the theme of a five-year program to strengthen the Grange and attract more young people.

CROWNING OF NATIONAL GRANGE PRINCE AND PRINCESS—In the pageantry which accompanies the Youth Recognition Activities at the National Grange Convention, the "Crowning Event" is the selection of the new National Grange Prince and Princess. Here are the 1966 winners, National Prince Steve Nygren of Colorado and National Princess Linda Settle of North Carolina.

Grange activities and ever-changing emphasis on community, national, and international needs and their solution or attainment, will continue to provide tremendous opportunities to young and old for personal growth. Can there be a finer tribute to this objective than a recent comment by a young Grange member:

> My life has been fuller; I have gained a greater sense of responsibility. I am able to talk before a group with more ease; and I have gained the friendship of many wonderful people.

The Junior Grange

The experience of belonging and participating can begin at age 5 in the Junior Grange. This unique organization, with its own special ritual and appropriate procedural outline for meetings, has been a regular activity of Subordinate Granges since the first juvenile Grange organizations were set up on a trial basis in a few states, and finally approved in the 1888 National Grange session. After studying the Texas Juvenile Grange Ritual, the Grange, in November 1890, adopted for all of the country a revised juvenile ritual that has stood the test of the years since and now is not only greatly influencing the 5-to-14 year olds to become better men and women but is giving them an organization "handle" to provide recreation, fun, and participation in many special community activities.

Junior Grange rules provide that membership terminates at age 14, the age at which that boy or girl becomes eligible to be a regular Subordinate Grange member and begin his degree work as a young adult. There is a provision, however, that junior members who have become junior Grangers at an early age may continue to be active until age 16, when they become members of the Subordinate Grange.

Thus the concept of the Founders is emphasized that while the 5-16 year olds have their own junior organization, from age 16 up they become participants in all *adult* Grange activities and carry on the early tradition that the Grange is truly a family organization. The sharing of experiences among all the age groups from 16 up in the Grange has been one of the factors that has held families together in rural areas. Today, much more attention must be given to this all over America to offset the fragmentation that divides families and which is now so apparent in our urban and, in some cases, suburban society.

With urban conditions in many places often breeding delinquency, trouble, frustration, and waste of opportunity, the Grange through its self-development activities is proving to be a "savior" of youth.

This statement by a Grange leader emphasizes the continuing interest in youth development:

> The Grange has been of incalculable value to the rural youth of America. It has been a teacher, a developer, a guiding force and a stimulating power. Here boys and girls have taken part in programs, in debates, in meetings with their parents and their elders. Here they have learned to do by doing. Here they have developed latent talents and have exercised their abilities; and here they have found that great thrill of "a chance to achieve" and to do things helpful and worthwhile. Many of the nation's leaders of today received valuable early training in the Grange a quarter of a century or more ago.

> **The greatest opportunity that the Grange offers young people is in its educational, fraternal and ritualistic work. Young people's degree teams, plays, choruses, orchestras, etc., have given ability and poise. The Grange Lecturer's Program has carried into practical life lessons begun in school and classroom. Here young people have been elected to office and have served their community and their state.**

> While the Grange has been of great value to young people, youth has equally blessed the Grange. They have brought vigor, enthusiasm, pep, energy, life and beauty into Grange meetings. They have helped to tie the family together and to make the Grange live and serve. More than one dormant and decadent Grange has been revived by the enthusiasm of youth.

> Just as the Grange is not a youth movement, so it is not an old people's organization, but rather the proper utilization of all the factors found in the well-rounded farm home and farm community. While the Grange has blessed and brightened the life and the future of farm boys and girls, from the very beginning, rural young people have helped and have improved the Grange.

> **One of the mightiest armies in America today is that of our youth. This young army can be an irresistible power for good if properly guided and directed, and the Grange offers peculiar advantages for usefulness and service.**

> We have countless special educational youth movements, organizations that will live and continually leave an indelible stamp for good on the Republic; besides various types of clubs and religious youth activities; but most of these mighty

armies lead our boys and girls to the door of opportunity and leave them there, except the Grange. It offers full membership, with equal voice and vote, to our young people while they are still young, and then extends a fraternal handclasp for the rest of their lives.

As long as the Grange has a continuing stream of boys and farm girls pausing before its altar for obligation and instruction, and as long as it holds these boys and girls through their mature years of life, it will never die, but will continue to serve and bless mankind.

What Youths Themselves Say About Grange Activities

No better proof of the worthiness and acceptance of the Grange Youth Program can be found than in the simply-stated, unrehearsed, deep-down feelings of Grange youth as they express it in reports, entry forms in contests, such as the Travel Scholarship, and other activities requiring a speech or written comment. Here are some examples of what Grange membership means:

The Grange is a way of life to me. We live a long way from the school I attend and I ride the school bus over 60 miles a day. Consequently, it is impossible for me to attend very many of the football, basketball, or other games. We live in the community where the Grange is located, so most of my outside activities are Grange centered. My lessons in singing at school have prepared me for vocal solos at Grange and the course in interpretive reading has helped me to be on the Lecturer's program whenever I am asked. In turn, *by being on Grange programs I have learned to think and speak on my feet so that I can be in school plays and give readings in contests without being so self-conscious.* I have been awarded a I in district and a II+ in state contests in plays and a II in our league on interpretive reading. I feel that the Grange helped me in this because it was there I first learned to face an audience.

✿　✿　✿　✿　✿

We hear so much of the lack of understanding between the "oldsters" and "youngsters" today but the Grange seems to bridge this gap by all of us working and playing together regardless of age. Also, in studying the history of the Grange, I have become very proud of the prominent part that rural people and the Grange have played in the growth of our America.

There are literally thousands of reports of how youths have improved their abilities, have "grown" in understanding and in appreciation of their patriotic and religious background. The whole "way of life" has been reorganized for the better! For example:

I joined the Grange just as soon as I could after I reached my 14th birthday. Even since I have been a member of the Grange, I have taken active part in the ritualism. I have studied the unwritten work and have studied the code. I believe that Grange ritualism is a very important part of the Grange life. When my Grange has guests, I always do things that will help to make them feel welcome to our meeting. My family and I have enjoyed the good times spent in visiting other Granges through the visitation project. Grange work is fellowship.

I participate in most all of the community service projects of our Grange and our Grange youth. Some of the things included on this are:

1. Water Safety. (Last summer and the summer before I assisted teaching the children to swim, and took the advanced swimming class.)

2. Toy Program. (Remaking toys for under-privileged children.)

3. Visited shut-ins in their homes, and took flowers and visited the rest home in our community.

4. Visited children's hospital (told stories to the children) and made tray favors.

5. Worked on the recreation area and Grange Hall. (Helped in clearing the woods and painting.)

6. Highway Safety Service. (I visited the Mayor's office to have a Safe Driving Proclamation signed; appeared on television twice and made a tape for radio; paraded on Gay Street in a box, and solicited signatures on Safe Driving pledges; visited 411 Speedway to encourage safe driving; participated in safe driving skits, and attended safety meetings.)

7. International Friendship. (Helped entertain international guests in our Grange.)

I feel I have helped the Grange to build a strong fraternal spirit for those of all ages by greeting and talking to as many members and visitors as possible during the Grange meeting evening. This form of fellowship helps many older folks in their personal life and helps them look forward to coming to Grange. The fellowship with the older members helps them to feel young in spirit once more. The fellowship with the younger members helps them in the many trials of their lives and helps give them some person to rely on in their many hours of need.

✿   ✿   ✿   ✿   ✿

I am constructing a table for the Grange Hall for use with phonograph and storing records. I worked 74 hours (in one year) collecting and repairing toys for the under-privileged children during the toy program project. I have enjoyed working on this project every year since I have been a Grange member and even before I became a member. I entertained an International guest in my home. Each time the Grange entertains groups of International students, one of my jobs is to furnish their transportation to and from the events.

Vital Role and Service of Lecturers

"We shall advance the cause of education among ourselves, and our children, by all just means within our power."
—*Declaration of Purposes.*

So deeply did the Founders believe the mission of the Grange to be one of emphasizing education as a major factor in the total Grange purpose and philosophy of "developing a fuller and richer rural life," that they added a special station in the officer structure of the Grange known as that of the *Worthy Lecturer.*

To Grange Lecturers was given the responsibility of "leading in the literary program and the educational work of the Grange" and thus "developing and directing to greater usefulness the latent abilities of your members."

Grange Lecturers have, therefore, over this century of service had a very substantial role in the evolution and progress of Rural America. They have made a contribution to the total program of work of the Grange— and to the lives, abilities, personal growth, and satisfaction of Grange members.

Dedicated and Inspired Devotion

Many indeed are the illustrations of dedicated and inspired devotion to this duty of Grange Lecturers to stimulate and inspire members of the Grange in their responsibility to each other—within the family—within the Grange—and within the community.

"As a man thinketh, so is he." To the extent that Grange Lecturers have, in various Subordinate Granges, accepted their full responsibility and have also been capable of enlisting the cooperation of Grange members, then so has that particular Grange been better equipped and more effectively motivated to carry out its purpose and develop a more significant program of work. The diligence and vision of the Grange Lecturer has, in many instances, influenced the total Grange membership, and helped to build Grange prestige.

Often the will and purpose of the entire Grange membership may be generated or modified in proportion to the effectiveness of the Lecturer's (literary and educational) program in "regular meetings." This will be no less important in the program of the Grange in the century ahead. New ideas and their development are an essential ingredient of positive and constructive action. Progress may be achieved out of such action.

Subordinate Grange Lecturers have been charged as recently as the current year to:

Lead in the educational program, and to recognize that we must, in the Grange, seek to correct the erroneous impression in the minds of many that education has become a function and a product of the public schools, colleges and universities alone. In the Grange we recognize that education is a continuous process, especially so in this rapidly changing world in which we are inescapably a part; and that

In a nation where we depend upon the citizens to make individual decisions daily, and collective decisions through the ballot system, education in the broadest concept becomes even more necessary.

The ultimate of education, however, must not be just job training. It must have as its objective the development of the humanities. There must be an understanding of history, literature, art, philosophies, etc.

Man is obligated to be concerned with the welfare of the human race. Therefore, our service to fellow-men must rate high.

Thus, Grange Lecturers become a very important part of the education system
of a democracy.

Throughout its entire 100 years, the Grange has been fortunate, too, in
having as National Lecturers men of outstanding ability, whose devotion
for the Order prompted a liberal expenditure of time, and *frequently,* the
sacrifice of important personal interests.

Duties of the Lecturer

Summarized, the duties of the Lecturer are:

1. To stimulate and develop the collective thinking of the members.
2. To be prepared with a program, with the above purpose in mind, as a vital
   function of each regular meeting, except those where election, degree work,
   and installation of officers are definitely scheduled, or where otherwise the
   Grange meeting is a full meeting without the Lecturer's program.
3. To encourage the young, and new members, to participate with all others in
   these programs and discussions.
4. To develop latent ability and challenge.
5. To incorporate subjects of international, national, state, and community interest, as well as topics regarding the home, farm and fields.
6. To assist members in knowing the Grange, local, state, and national history,
   policies, legislative goals, and purposes.
7. To encourage cooperation with the Pomona Granges and the Subordinate
   Granges within Pomona jurisdiction.
8. To know and take appropriate account of state and national Grange Lecturer
   suggestions.
9. To help develop and participate in County, State, District, and Regional
   Conferences to stimulate each other.

To Develop a Higher Manhood and Womanhood Among Ourselves

One of the real opportunities—and obligations of the Grange Lecturer,
which has been met exceedingly well over this century, is to help the
individual grow in mind and purpose. The fraternal atmosphere of Grange
meetings extends to Grange Lecturers' unique privileges and opportunities; even as the plant grows and develops in the proper climate and in
fertile soil.

It is in this climate and this fraternal structure that Grange Lecturers
have been peculiarly successful in many cases in encouraging the young
and the difficult to become writers, readers, and speakers in the Grange
meetings. Hence, Granges and Grange members have developed leadership, and have directed that leadership into greater usefulness, in and out
of the Grange.

13

Unique Activities
of Women

In 1867, the legal status of women was about the same as that of the then recently-freed slaves. The Founders of the Grange took exception to this attitude within the organization which they visualized.

As related in Chapter 2, they took the then unprecedented step of deciding and acting immediately to put women on an equal status with men in the Grange. They thereby created an unique family organization—the first in history to give women a high place in the sphere of things, sharing equally the most exalted positions of the Grange with her "brother." The Grange structure from the very beginning has likewise given women responsibilities commensurate with their abilities and privileges.

So it is that over the years, this basic decision of the Founders has proved to be one of the more important strengthening factors of the Grange.

DR. JONAS SALK, Director of the Salk Institute for Biological Studies, pointing out to Mrs. Alta Peck, Chairman, Grange Home Economics Department, progress on construction ·of the Salk Institute, San Diego, Calif. Grange women raised over $14,000 and a room in the Institute has been named the Grange Seminar Room.

Home Economics Emphasis—A Better Grange

In 1867, plenty of work was found for the gentler sex. Not only did they handle the "homemaking" functions of the Grange Hall, and in Grange meetings the embellishment of the decorations and arrangement of ornaments by the proper placing of the flowers of nature and the important food and social functions usually expected of women then, but they did far more than this.

GRANGE WOMEN AID LESS FORTUNATE PEOPLE OF PHILIPPINES—*turning over HEC Grange donations of tools for community development (through CARE) to local officials, school teachers, and other leaders and citizens.*

They demonstrated their abilities as Lecturers, as officers at other stations, and as committee chairmen and members. They took the leadership in community and in youth activities that have characterized the beginning and the entire life of the Grange and its program.

Better homemaking became a vital feature of Grange programs and activities. This later led to the appointment of a permanent Committee on Home Economics in the National Grange in 1910, which was then described as follows:

> Home Economics stands for all the touches of home life—the structure of the house, its furnishings, equipment, management and sanitary care, the care and training of the children, the purchase and preparation of food, and everything else that pertains to the work of homemaking.

EMBROIDER WITH A PURPOSE — National Grange Home Economics Chairman Alta Peck of Litchfield, Conn., congratulates Mrs. G. Wallace Caulk, who accepted a $100 award for a Grange woman in Delaware who won "best of show" in the Grange historical sampler contest in 1965. Mrs. Caulk is the wife of the Delaware State Master.

It is surely the duty of the Grange to become more active in furthering this work among its members. We recommend that State Granges especially should emphasize this work and furnish good speakers for their State, Pomona, and Subordinate meetings, to arouse interest in the study of the home.

Encourage exhibits at State and County Fairs to be as educational and helpful in matters of improved homemaking as in agriculture and livestock; to let everything be shown that would tend to uplift the home and its surroundings.

Since 1911, then, Home Economics has been a major activity within the Grange. The National Home Economics Committee, creating ideas and helping State, Pomona and Subordinate Granges to build and carry on outstanding programs, has been working with earnest and dedicated women who have contributed more toward building Grange into a stronger force throughout rural America than possibly could have been done in any other than the truly family structure. The report of the Home Economics Committee is a scheduled and required item in the order of business of the "regular" Subordinate Grange meeting.

So important has the Home Economics work by women become that by vote of the National Grange, official regalia has been provided, or authorized. Often the Home Economics Committee is called upon to furnish, or participate in, the literary and educational program of the Grange Lecturers. Normally, the Home Economics Committee participates in most of the total balanced program of activities of the Grange . . . its community service program, in its work with school and educational authorities in community, county, state, and throughout the nation.

The women of the Grange, through their Home Economics activities, have contributed immeasurably to most of the more worthwhile projects and activities of the Grange as a whole. It would indeed be impossible to have a balanced *Grange program* without a reasonably effective "women's work" or Home Economics program of activities.

GRANGE WOMEN CARE — A long-standing feature of the Grange women's home economics program is the Grange-CARE project to supply hand water pumps to South American countries. To provide fresh water and improve the health of these people, Grange women have contributed over $15,000 since the Grange involvement started.

THE GRANGE HELPS — The 1964 March of Dimes child is greeted by National Grange Home Economics Chairman Mrs. Alta Peck of Litchfield, Conn., at a regional March of Dimes meeting in New York City. Grange members, led by Grange women, contribute huge sums each year to philanthropic groups.

Mobilizing Women's Talents Today

Capable Grange women are a major force today both in building a stronger and better rural America and stronger, more active, more effective Granges, as well as promoting international understanding.

Necessarily diversified, the Home Economics program today includes:

1. **Projects for membership building,** and for greater pride and joy in membership.

2. **Projects for community service**—long-range and emergency aid. (See Chapter 14 for heartwarming stories of this type of service.)

3. **Projects for more appreciation of the Grange**—such projects as the Memorial Library in the National Grange Building in Washington, D.C.; various fund-raising projects for local organizations, and beautification projects.

4. **Projects to aid the less fortunate people of the world.** Examples: "Canning Jars to Greece;" "Self-Helps to the Philippines," such as agricultural hand tools, woodworking kits, physical education kits, sewing machines, and medical aid kits; "Medico in Cambodia." A current project is "Community Water Pumps to Latin America" to provide fresh water and to combat disease.

5. **Projects for the home and family,** such as: *Home safety programs*—"No Falls" promotion and "Fireproof Your Family." *Educational programs,* such as: Consumer Credit, Care of Fabrics, Deceptive Packaging, Home Decoration, Flower Arrangement, and Color in the Home.

6. **Health Cooperative Programs** with all health agencies, the promotion of which includes such educational and financial projects as a special national project to raise funds for the Salk Institute for Biological Studies in which a room is named for the Grange. Over $14,000 was contributed for this Grange Seminar Room.

7. **Debt Retirement** which continues to provide funds to reduce the debt on the National Grange headquarters building. Thereby, funds from building rental receipts will be released for all other phases of the total Grange program.

Contests

Contests to create interest in Home Economics Department activities include: (1) *National Grange All-Cotton Sewing Contest* with approximately 50,000 Grange and non-Grange contestants; *National Grange Needlework Contest* with competition in crocheting, knitting, and embroidery; (3) *Sampler Contest* to bring to the attention of the women the One Hundredth Anniversary of the Grange and promote historical appreciation; and (4) the *Flag Contest* to obtain a design for an official Grange flag. And there have been many others.

NEBRASKA WOMAN WINS GRANGE SEWING CONTEST—Mrs. Max Eberspacher of Beaver Crossing, Neb., models the two-piece cranberry jacket dress which won her top honors in the $25,000 National Grange All-Cotton Sewing Contest.

TEENAGER WINS YOUTH SEWING CONTEST—Miss Carol Klock, 14, of Troutdale, Ore., models her prize-winning sleeveless gingham dress, which placed first in the youth category of the 9th annual $25,000 National Grange All-Cotton Sewing Contest.

14

What the Grange Stands for in

Community Service

"Because we met the needs of others,
our lives have been enriched."
—*A Granger's comment*

Unselfish Service to Others

Grange members for nearly 100 years have been known far and wide for their unselfish, practical community service which has made the lives of others happier and better—has often turned discouragement to comfort and hope—and has improved the appearance, supplied added conveniences, and advanced in a hundred or a thousand ways their communities as better places in which to live.

This very day, thousands of Grange members in hundreds of Subordinate Grange communities, some with publicity and some so quietly that few if any know about it, are making the lives of their neighbors and fellow citizens brighter with lighter burdens, as well as conducting community progress programs, creating new facilities and structures and improving old ones for the benefit of all.

X-RAY MACHINE—Purchased by Farmers Enterprise Grange No. 165 (N. J.) for the Health Clinic.

ADDITION TO CHURCH—Work being done by volunteers from Hebron Grange No. 1228 (Washington County, N. Y.) who donated: 409 work hours, $746.64.

OPENING GAME IN GRANGE-BUILT BALL PARK—From a field to a Little League ball park in 60 days of hard work by members of No. Stonington Grange No. 138 (New London County, Conn.).

VOLUNTEERS PLAY SANTA CLAUS —Members of Volunteer Grange, Knoxville, Tennessee, played Santa Claus for 238 children in 54 families. Nearly 100% of the Grange members, as well as nonmembers, helped in this project which included remaking and refinishing hundreds of toys.

Ever since the Grange was founded in 1867, the practical projects of its Patrons are tangible evidence of community spirit among its young and old. Thousands of volunteers have put countless hours and immeasurable personal resources into this work, and have done it with pleasure and a spirit of friendliness, dedication, and regard for others.

Because the Subordinate Granges are made up of people who have common interests in their local community and area, and because the Grange is truly a family organization, it is well fitted to perform this community service. No other farm organization and few community groups have the assets in people, in knowledge, and in spirit, as well as declared organization purpose, to carry on this type of work.

The methods of community improvement, betterment, and neighbor-serving projects are literally unlimited, and vary from community to community as Grange members work together to "provide leadership for community improvement where leadership is lacking; to support other leadership where such support is the greater need."

The Community Progress Program

Incentive for this work began early in Grange history. The very first activities of Grange members were designed to help each other, their neighbors, and their community—this later developing into a National Grange Principle through state and national promotion and incentives.

In 1927, Honor Grange specifications were set up by the National Grange, which presented Award Achievement Certificates to Subordinate Granges meeting definite community service requirements.

Then came the splendid Community Service Program in 1947, known since 1964 as the *Community Progress Program*, which has resulted in new high records of achievement due to outstanding support, promotion, and incentive activities of the national contest co-sponsored by the National Grange and Sears-Roebuck Foundation.

Recognition of projects that contribute to making a community a better place in which to live and work is the aim of the current jointly sponsored program in which State Contests and finally the national awards have been featured.

The 1966-67 program invites Subordinate Granges to submit entries up to June 1, 1967 of well-conceived projects that contribute to community life and welfare. Included in the challenge to all Granges are suggestions that they consider, in the light of today's conditions, one or more of the following:

> Projects to increase employment and income—the expansion and development of rural industries and more productive agriculture.
>
> Projects to aid in serving your people with better schools, health, sanitation, communication, protection, and recreation, and old age comforts.
>
> Projects to improve the living environment, appearance, and culture of your community.
>
> Projects to develop the youth, the adults, and the families of the less fortunate and disadvantaged.

Examples of Tremendous Accomplishments

In a booklet entitled, *The Contest Everybody Wins*, Donald S. Stroetzel tells the story of one year's activities of Granges in the Community Progress Program. His dramatic story of the activities of more than 275,000 Grangers tells how they contributed four million man-hours of volunteer labor to community projects—enough, if concentrated, to build an entire city of 2,000 homes.

From other reports, the following excerpts were selected. However, to the thousands of Grangers who unselfishly sacrifice countless hours of personal time and personal expenditures, it seems rather unfair to be unable to tell here what they have done and are doing, and to properly thank them and commend them for their efforts. So, the examples cited are merely suggestive of what many, many other Grange groups have done, and are doing, to accomplish something badly needed in their community, namely *a rebirth of community pride, and a new recognition of both individual and organizational responsibility.*

Union (Ohio) Grange No. 1648

Major changes in the lives of so many rural people, as urbanization spreads, is highlighted in this right-from-the-heart statement in the Community Progress Report of Union Grange No. 1648, Richland County, Shelby, Ohio:

The founders of Union Grange had the Grange home very well located on a knoll easily seen by the surrounding countryside and four and one-half miles from the nearest town which has a population of 10,000. The community has made many radical changes since the Grange was founded in March, 1906. The schools in the vicinity have been absorbed in the city system and many of the rural church members have been absorbed by the city churches. *The Grange stands alone to hold the interest of our rural people and keep alive their love of nature and interest in our open country.*

Owing to the close proximity of the expanding industrial centers around Mansfield and Shelby the problems of the community are changing and more and more farmers are converting into part-time farmers and there is an influx of urban people into the section which until recently was purely rural population and depended entirely upon the farm for its livelihood.

The aim of our community service program is to aid in helping improve living conditions, to promote peace and fellowship throughout the world, to cooperate with schools, churches, and other organizations which have the same program.

A total of 337 members worked many long hours in service to our community; 267 non-members and our junior members have also contributed much to the programs.

We hope that through our Community Service activities we not only are doing good today but also that we are making our youth conscious of the needs of the community and are impressing them with the fact that much can be done about meeting these needs by working together through an organization.

This Grange is a real community force. It has converted 80 acres of farmland for the entire county to enjoy as a recreation area. It has helped build a $32,000 lodge. It sends Christmas checks of $5 to every member of the Armed Services and pays their Grange dues for as long as they are in the service. It provides an annual $100 scholarship to a graduating senior for study in agriculture, home economics, or to become a vet or a nurse. It has built a splendid $25,000 dining hall which it makes available for community meetings of the Chamber of Commerce, railroad employees, agricultural groups, civic clubs, and other organizations.

Its adoption of a Korean orphan encouraged others to do likewise. Its Junior Grange followed their elder's example by supporting an Indian boy from Cherokee Indian Mission at Oaks, Okla.

There are countless other examples of most unusual service projects that have had a tremendous impact on the lives and fortunes of neighbors and other citizens in the area.

FIRST STEP TO A BEAUTIFUL GRANGE HALL —Members of the Building Committee of the Volunteer Grange Knoxville, Tennessee, working and planning. Their fund was enriched more than $5,000, in 1960, when Volunteer won 2nd place in the nation in the Community Service contest.

ANOTHER OUTSTANDING GRANGE COMMUNITY ACTIVITY—*This giant check for $38,164.30, the contribution of Grange Members was presented to Dr. Hans Waine (center), medical director of the Massachusetts Chapter, Arthritis Foundation, at the Massachusetts State Grange Annual Session. (L to r) Mrs. Alice E. M. Marshall, chairman of the Grange arthritis research program; Ralph G. Boyd, member governing board of National Arthritis Foundation, and Waldo M. Chamberlain (right), chairman of the Grange "Aids To Independence" program for arthritis patients. Mrs. Alta Peck, national Home Economics Chairman, represented Herschel Newsom at the ceremonies.*

Flowing Well (Nebr.) Grange No. 396

Flowing Well Grange No. 396, in Beaver Crossing, Nebr., revived Main Street in their community. Their small Grange Hall, built many years ago, was recently replaced by a new hall which was so outstanding compared to other nearby buildings that it motivated others along Main Street to make improvements, thus beautifying the whole business community.

Patrons of this Grange also cleared 16 bad corners of plum brush and volunteer tree growth to provide a clearer view and reduce accidents. The ladies made warm covers for orphan children, collected hundreds of old pairs of glasses, conducted a Diabetic Protection Program, sponsored a 12 months' Farmhouse and Highway Safety Program, staged a teachers reception, worked on a long-range plan to build up doctor service in the area, provided rural vacations for city children, and helped collect clothing for needy children in other parts of the world.

Vashon-Maury (Wash.) Grange No. 1105

Vashon-Maury Grange No. 1105 of King County, Washington, was instrumental in greatly improving telephone service to 1400 subscribers on Vashon Island in Puget Sound. They helped long-suffering subscribers get better service, have their deposits returned which had been held for years, forced the telephone company to agree to provide repair service on a 7-day 24-hour-a-day basis, provide toll slips for long distance charges, and make improvements in lines and equipment. This Grange also fought high ferryboat tolls for pickup trucks, and won the battle when fares were reduced.

Antelope Gap (Wyo.) Grange No. 60

Another Grange—Antelope Gap No. 60, at Wheatland, Wyoming, consisted of only 25 families. After eight years of effort this Grange finally put on the spurt that brought telephone service to the area. Fifteen Grange members worked 2428 hours or 303 man-days in all kinds of weather to put up 32 miles of poles and telephone lines. To help the men, Grange wives served meals at the Grange Hall and in the field.

HOW ANTELOPE GAP (Wyo.) Grange No. 60 members put up 32 miles of poles and telephone lines to bring the first telephone service to the area.

BEAUTIFUL RECREATIONAL PAVILION—project of Hamden (Conn.) Grange No. 99—Grange members engaged in many activities to earn thousands of dollars making possible Brooksvale Recreation Park, a community center on 100 acres of country ground including this beautiful pavilion.

Hamden (Conn.) Grange No. 99

Here is what a community Grange at New Haven, Conn., has done for its neighbors. Hamden Grange No. 99 meets in the Parish House of a community church. Its 239 members are mostly employed *outside agriculture.* They are but one example of what is happening throughout America in that worthy people will congregate together in an organization like the Grange because it provides "that certain something" people want and need in the way of a Center, whose program and ideals encourage them to want to participate. This is another case proving that Americans will gravitate to where there is an inspiring program and dedicated leadership which encourages them to donate their time and talents to the service of others.

As a result of Hamden Grange No. 99 Patrons having the dream of a community recreation center, they developed 100 acres of country land into Brooksvale Recreation Park with a beautiful recreational pavilion. This four-year project included Grangers providing $3459.94 out of $5839.74, which the project cost. In one year, Grangers donated 1,000 hours of work for poison ivy eradication, making and marking trails, clearing camp sites, building shelters, feeding birds, and planting shrubs and trees.

Spencer (N.Y.) Grange No. 1110

In the Community Service Contest, emphasis has been placed on the effort of the Grange members in a "do-it-yourself" type of program. This new concept of Community Progress is built on the idea that the entire community should be involved in establishing goals and carrying out the projects. Grange leadership in uniting the organizations and agencies then becomes a major criteria.

Spencer Grange, No. 1110, in Tioga County, New York, serves as an excellent example.

Spencer is a small rural community of 800 residents, formerly dependent upon the agricultural economy. With consolidation of the better farms, and the elimination of the marginal farms, many of the people found employment in nearby educational and industrial communities.

Joint meetings with the Chamber of Commerce of Spencer, Operation Advance groups (an Extension sponsored program), and individuals revealed seven areas of concern: (1) Industrial Development, (2) Planning, (3) Natural Resource Utilization and Tourism, (4) Vocational Education,

MOTIVATING GRANGE MOTIVATORS — The Master of Spencer (N.Y.) Grange No. 1110 receives a check for $10,000 from Robert V. Mullen, Director of Youth and Rural Activities, The Sears-Roebuck Foundation, (left) and National Master Herschel D. Newsom (center).

(5) Local Recreation, (6) Public Utilities and Governmental Services, and (7) Community Appearance. Eight major and six minor projects developed from these concerns.

One of the major projects involved transforming a swamp in the center of Spencer into a beautiful eight-acre lake. An island reached by a bridge adds to the scenic beauty, as does the park area, equipped with fireplaces and picnic tables. Over 8,000 man-hours of volunteer labor went into this one project, as well as $11,000 collected locally.

Plans for the future include a band stand, a bird sanctuary, a live biology laboratory for school children, and an open-air theater for nature lecturers.

The Grange helped a local industry double their floor space; secured an expressway; formed a $50,000 stock corporation; have a draft for a zoning ordinance; awarded $100 Vocational Scholarships to 15 students; sponsored a Mariner Scout Troop and Cub Pack and carried out several other projects.

Of Spencer Grange's 149 members, 67 per cent or 100, took an active part in the Community Progress Program, as did 897 nonmembers. Community pride has been developed, community goals established, and community unity secured.

The village of Spencer has a future because of the leadership of Spencer Grange in the Community Progress Program.

It has been well said that Grange activities such as these are practical demonstrations of Democracy in action.

FOR AN ALL-AROUND PROGRAM OF UNSELFISH COMMUNITY IMPROVEMENT — Master Joseph G. Wild and Mrs. Wild of the Spencer Grange No. 1110, Spencer, N. Y. naturally proudly display the evidence of Spencer's outstanding activities which placed it first among 4,500 Subordinate Granges entered in the 1964-65 Community Progress program sponsored by the National Grange and Sears-Roebuck Foundation.

15

What the Grange
Stands for in

Farm Legislation,
Policies and Programs

With great wisdom, the Grange Founders took every possible step, and its Declaration of Purposes adopted in February of 1874, makes the emphatic statement that the Grange is not to be or to become a partisan or party organization.

However, both the Founders, and subsequent leadership, strongly pointed out that by becoming a Patron of Husbandry no member gives up "that inalienable right and duty, that belongs to every American citizen, to take a proper interest in the politics of his country."

Over the years, even though politicians sought to become Grange members by calling themselves farmers, and attempted to involve the Order in partisan matters, Grange leaders kept above strictly party entanglements and led their members carefully and thoughtfully on the basis of principles, duly established. Thus have Grange recommendations become highly sought after by legislative and executive officials, becoming an important force in both administrative and legislative development—for the benefit not only of the farmers but for all Americans.

Early in the fight to keep the Grange non-partisan but to build its prestige as a strong force for good legislation, National Master James Draper in 1886, after a particularly severe test of Grange principles, had this to say:

> A national farmers' organization without the power to discuss the political rights of its members would be a farce beneath the dignity of intelligent men. The farmers want an organization that will use its influence upon the legislatures, state and national, to protect the rights of their members; and no organization can long maintain standing with them if it does not render such assistance.
>
> We have been adopting resolutions and petitions long enough and to little effect. Let us try the remedy that has been suggested at nearly every session of the National Grange; let us, with our ballots, send men to the legislatures, state

THE ORIGINAL ALBERT S. GOSS Conference Room at 744 Jackson Place, Washington, D.C., was also the site of many important legislative and other conferences. This group of State Grange Masters, who were members of the Board of Directors of the National Grange Monthly, met with Ezra Taft Benson, (seventh from left) then U.S. Secretary of Agriculture, other U.S.D.A. officials, and National Master Newsom.

and national, who will equalize and reduce taxation; restrain corporations from oppressing the people; keep our public domain for actual settlers; have the finances managed in the interest of the people; prevent gamblers from pricing our productions, and extend the same protection to the farmer and to the manufacturer.

For this great work the Grange was organized, and it was not born to die nor will it fail in the accomplishment of its purpose.

What the Grange Stands for in Basic Farm Policies

Each year Grange headquarters produces a "Summary of Legislative Policies and Programs" which outlines the National Grange position on every segment of agricultural development and growth, as well as Grange policy on matters of International Relations, Resource Development and Use, National Welfare, Education, Economic Matters, Health, and Transportation. It will be seen that Grange interest is not confined strictly to matters affecting the rural population, but is equally directed toward the well-being of all citizens and their general prosperity.

There are certain basic policies with which the Grange has been identified throughout its 100-year history.

The Grange seeks to obtain public recognition that agriculture is the foundation upon which much of the growth, progress, and development of our country has been built. U.S. agriculture supplies the American people with the most abundant, varied, and nutritious food supply to be found in the world; and at the lowest percentage of the consumer's spendable income in the history of the world. At the same time, it produces many of the raw materials which feed the world's largest industrial machine.

The Family Farm—Its Preservation

The Grange has long recognized the family farm as the backbone of American agriculture, and indeed our democratic society. A primary objective of the Grange is to preserve the family-type farm—individual enterprise—operation.

By Grange interpretation such an operation should:

(a) Place major reliance upon the farm family for both labor and management;

(b) Function on capital provided at the risk of the operator;

(c) Provide full-time productive employment to the family;

(d) Provide to the operating family its major source of income;

(e) Utilize modern labor-saving devices and other practices which contribute to efficiency; and

(f) Enable the family farm operator to earn and receive—for his labor, management and investment—a return which is reasonably comparable to that received for those engaged in other legitimate segments of the American economy.

Other Current Farm Policies

MONOPOLY IN AGRICULTURE

The continuing trend toward larger farms and fewer owners may be an economic necessity in order to create a viable agriculture. However, any acceleration of the trends toward the industrialized corporation-type farm will be viewed with grave concern by the Grange. This trend, if carried to the extreme, will establish a capitalistic monopoly and enable a few to exercise almost complete control over the majority, thereby weakening our democratic system and creating a threat to the economy of abundance which has blessed our Nation.

While vigorously reaffirming support for the capitalistic individual enterprise system, Grange policy declares that:

"The full fruits of this system can be more widely realized when opportunities, incentives, and rewards of enterprise are dispersed over a wide range of ownership."

COLLEGE STUDENTS SEEK GRANGE VIEWPOINT — Grange Legislative Representative Harry L. Graham discusses farm and rural problems with students from American University in Washington, D. C. Grange officials are called upon frequently by other colleges across the nation to tell about the Grange and the reasons for its positions on legislative matters.

SUPPLY CONTROL AND MANAGEMENT

To a reasonable degree, the supply of farm commodities must be brought into balance with the actual needs of the Nation including its foreign commitments. Programs resulting in buildups of excessively large government-owned stocks represent wasteful and unsound public policy.

Producers themselves must face their responsibility for effective control and management of their production if they are to receive an equitable income resulting from a balance between supply and demand in the market place. It is the responsibility of producers to assist government in the development of such programs—when needed—and to abide by provisions of the program once they are developed and approved by producers through democratic procedures.

CERTIFICATE PROGRAM FOR WHEAT

The domestic parity wheat certificate program was developed and first recommended by the National Grange, which has, in cooperation with other wheat and commodity groups, and general farm organizations, succeeded in writing the program into law in the 1964 Farm Bill and in extending it to a 4-year program in the Food and Agriculture Act of 1965.

FEED GRAINS PROGRAMS

A balanced production of meat and animal products, the proper functioning of other farm commodity programs, and the expansion and protection of our foreign trade depends, to a large extent on a realistic program for the production, storage, and sale of feed grains stocks. The Grange, therefore, developed the feed grains provisions which were incorporated in the Food and Agriculture Act of 1965.

DAIRY POLICY

The Grange sought the passage of the Class I Base Dairy Surplus Program for federal milk marketing areas as included in Title I of the 1965 farm bill. This program protects the pooling provisions of the order by allocating to each producer his historic share of the Class I market, with the return for this production separately computed. The producer may thus eliminate that part of his production which goes into the market at the lower or "surplus" price without reducing his share of the Class I market.

The Grange will support the approval of this program in any federal milk marketing order area where the need has been established.

FOREIGN MARKET DEVELOPMENT PROGRAMS

The Grange supports the foreign market development programs developed by commodity groups. These programs expand our dollar cash sales in foreign markets and have hearty endorsement of the Grange.

New and expanded foreign markets for our agricultural commodities should be aggressively developed by full use of the 5% set aside which the Congress has earmarked for that purpose out of foreign currencies derived from Title I, PL 480 sales.

COTTON

The National Grange urges:
1. The return at the earliest practicable date to the parity principle in determining cotton price support;
2. The Secretary of Agriculture to encourage ASCS committees in cotton counties to request that cotton acreage be excluded from cropland adjustment contracts; and,
3. Amendments to the Food and Agriculture Act of 1965 to exempt cotton allotments of 10 acres or less from cropland adjustment programs.

16

What the Grange
Stands for in

Encouraging
Private Enterprise

"Except for the Granger Laws regulating monopolies
and the Grange's sponsorship of cooperatives, America
might well have gone the road to Communism."
—Raymond W. Miller

The farmer has always been an individualist. Not only has he been required to face and overcome the challenges of nature in his operations, but he has been forced to show a special brand of independence in his business operations to achieve a livelihood. Over the years he has been beset by business problems, often being victimized because of his lack of knowledge, his gullibility, and his lack of defense.

So it was that in the late 1860's when the Grange was conceived, and its Founders had the dream of an organization that would protect his interests, fight for his rights, and help him act with others to buy together, sell together, and work together for mutual protection and advancement, he enthusiastically became a member of the Grange.

Grange Championed Private Enterprise System

From the very beginning, through its Declaration of Purposes, the Grange championed the private or individual enterprise system. Great stress was laid on the preservation of the integrity of property rights as well as the integrity of the rights of labor, and above all, support of the profit incentive, so much a part of our American capitalistic system.

In his classic book, *Can Capitalism Compete?* Raymond W. Miller quotes Herbert Hoover, before he became President of the United States, in "a most significant analysis of the genius of North American freedom in developing the most highly productive economy in the world."

This is what Mr. Hoover said in defining the American Social System:

> We have, in fact, a special social system of our own. We have made it ourselves from materials brought in revolt from conditions in Europe. We have lived it; we constantly improve it; we have seldom tried to define it. It abhors autocracy and does not argue with it, but fights it. It is not capitalism, or socialism, or syndicalism, nor a cross breed of them. Like most Americans, I refuse to be damned by anybody's "word-classification" of it, such as "capitalism," "Plutocracy," "proletariat" or "middle class," or any other, or to any kind of compartment that is based on the assumption of some group dominating somebody else.
>
> The social force in which I am interested is far higher and far more precious a thing than all these. It springs from something infinitely more enduring; it springs from the one source of human progress—that each individual shall be given the chance and stimulation for development of the best within which he has been endowed in heart and mind; it is the sole source of progress; it is American individualism.
>
> The rightfulness of our individualism can rest either on philosophic, political, economic, or spiritual grounds. It can rest on the ground of being the only safe avenue to further human progress.

> —*American Individualism*
> Herbert Hoover, pp. 12-13,
> Copyright, 1952 by Doubleday & Co., Inc.

Today the philosophy of Grange leaders continues to emphasize the importance and value of our private or individual enterprise system. Recent words of the National Master, Herschel D. Newsom, in dedicating the beautiful new California State Grange Headquarters in Sacramento, in June, 1966, emphatically make this point:

> We must insist that not only our own government but all governments of the world, must take reasonable steps to preserve the integrity of property and job . . .
>
> There must be progress and growth, without destruction of carefully and accurately defined *property rights* and employment rights. This kind of growth and progress will extend and enhance opportunity for individuals who may be incited to improve themselves as we seek always to use the very strength which this American system of reasonably regulated capitalism has given us as Americans and as members of the Grange.
>
> This, indeed, has been the basic American and Grange philosophy which has improved and extended the opportunities of individuals in America. It is this system by which America has developed and achieved a posture that now imposes even greater responsibilities on the Grange, as well as all Americans.
>
> We should seek as best we may to literally help to influence the pattern of increasing opportunity for human beings, of improving integrity of investment and security in personal employment in the rest of the world, so that the rest of the world may, in turn, assume its full measure of responsibility to all people.
>
> We dare not depart from the fundamental precept of prime recognition for the dignity and the integrity, with responsibility, of the individual. Neither, however, can we ignore the fundamental principle that "the whole can never become greater than the sum of all its parts." Therefore, to whatever extent we fail to provide the stimulation for individual enterprise—carefully guarding and protecting the legitimate rights of individuals to achieve comparable growth and progress—we inevitably will diminish the growth and progress of any people, anywhere in the world.

Grange Creates, Promotes Cooperatives

In the interestingly written history of cooperatives by Martin A. Abrahamsen, Acting Administrator, Farmer Cooperative Service, U.S.D.A., *Agriculture Cooperation—Pioneer to Modern,* he credits the Grange with important contributions to the creation, growth, and organization of cooperative purchasing and marketing organizations. He says:

> Early Granges assembled farmer-members' orders and placed them with dealers who shipped carloads of supplies direct to farmers. Price concessions were obtained from suppliers for performing these services. In the years 1871-76, more than 20,000 local Granges, as well as some 26 state agency systems, were established. County Granges in many cases acted as business enterprises for members of the local units.
>
> In 1874, the National Grange sent a representative to Europe to gather information about cooperation. As a result, the Grange began to sponsor the organization of business cooperatives.
>
> An early writer on cooperation said: "The great contribution of the National Grange was the formulation and distribution in 1875, of a set of rules for the organization of cooperative stores. These rules were based on those of 28 weavers of Rochdale. . . ." (The Rochdale Equitable Pioneers Society, organized in 1844, was the first consumer cooperative in Rochdale, England.)
>
> Many cooperative Grange stores were organized in Michigan, Maine, New York, Kansas, Texas, and California. They sold groceries and clothing as well as general farm supplies, hardware, and agricultural implements. These were more successful than the earlier Grange organizations, which sold goods below going prices or distributed savings on the basis of stockholdings . . .

An important contribution of the Grange was its demonstration that the Rochdale type of cooperative, which handled goods at prevailing prices and distributed net savings according to patronage, offered the most promising basis for sound cooperative efforts.

Over the years, and today, the Grange strongly supports marketing, purchasing, and service cooperatives.

Latest Grange legislative policy makes the strong point that if the individual family-type farm operation is to remain in existence, it will be necessary to continue the development of stronger and better cooperatives to provide the essential bargaining power which this type of operator must have in order to compete.

The Grange fights efforts to cripple cooperatives through punitive taxation or court actions and works for legislation to provide that cooperatives have the same privileges as other businesses to merge and acquire competing businesses.

It gives full support to rural electric cooperatives and to using REA facilities to make adequate telephone service available to rural people. It recommends cooperation with CUNA, international and state credit union leagues and promotes the organization of Grange credit unions throughout the country.

Saving Insurance Dollars for Members

It was but natural that in its promotion of the cooperative idea, with an organization doing for its participants what they couldn't do for themselves individually, Grange leaders looked on insurance protection as a logical service to provide members.

Early in Grange history, its leaders felt that fire insurance was costing farmers too much; and that Grange members because of devotion to family and home were a preferred risk and entitled to lower costs on the most complete and inclusive insurance coverage possible. As a result, they organized and promoted cooperative or mutual fire insurance companies. With literally hundreds of successes in that field, Grange leaders went on later to provide mutual automobile and casualty insurance, life insurance, all kinds of liability insurance for the home, farm or business, fidelity bonds, and more recently the modern package-policy such as Homeowners, Farmowners, and Commercial Multi-Peril policies.

The comprehensive protection and tremendous savings write another chapter in the outstanding service record of the Grange for its members.

Five of these Grange insurance companies have multi-state operations, and have close affiliation with the National Grange, reporting regularly to the Annual Session. Details about their operations, and of their reinsurance company, are given below. Several hundred other insurance companies serving Grange members operate within a single state, county or Pomona Grange jurisdiction.

Farmers and Traders Life Insurance Company, of Syracuse, N. Y.

The National Grange itself took the necessary specific action and indeed with effective support and participation by State Granges of New York, Pennsylvania, and Ohio, raised the required original capital in 1912 to organize its own life insurance company, first known as Farmers National Life Insurance Company. Soon after the company began business in 1914, the name was changed to the present one.

To comply with the insurance laws of New York, and because the capital requirements were beyond the reach of the Grange in those days,

ARCHITECT'S drawing of how Syracuse, N. Y. Headquarters of Farmers and Traders Life Insurance Company will look when addition at right is completed in 1966.

it was originally organized as a stock company, but with a plan to mutualize it so that it will to 100% owned by Grange members and the other policyholders for whom it provides life insurance service. This mutualization program began in 1954. It is almost completed. When realized, probably in 1967, this will be another of the long-term plans and objectives accomplished during the "First Century of Service and Evolution" of the Grange.

Although the Company was organized primarily to serve Grange and rural people, it now serves people in all walks of life. It does, however, keep a close tie with its sponsoring organization for a majority of its directors are present and past state and national Grange officers.

Today this life insurance company, proud of its 52 years of growth, and service, has assets over $66 million, offers a multiple and broad service to both urban and rural communities in 27 states and the District of Columbia, with more than $250 million of insurance in force. Its President, Matthias E. Smith, has served as an officer in Subordinate, Pomona, and New York State Granges. He follows the late and revered Alvin E. Hanson, President of the Company from March, 1961 to December, 1965.

National Grange Mutual Insurance Co., Keene, N. H.

The National Grange Mutual Insurance Co., Keene, N.H., was organized in 1923 as the "National Grange Mutual Liability Co." Sponsored by the Grange, it wrote auto insurance for Grange members. Presently its charter permits the underwriting of all lines of insurance except life insurance and annuities.

In 1923, the company was licensed in New Hampshire only and its gross premium volume was $11,231,95. Today, with a premium volume of $38,985,029.63, NGM operates in 22 states and the District of Columbia, and ranks 24th among the nation's 2,230 mutual casualty and property insurers. It has assets over $65 million, and a policyholders surplus over $19 million.

NGM purchased the assets and in-force business of the National Grange Fire Insurance Co. in 1958 and adopted its present name.

HOME of National Grange Mutual Insurance Company, Keene, N. H.

NGM's home office, with 54,000 square feet of floor space and housing over 300 employees, was opened in 1950. An addition, which will more than double this space, is currently under construction. Branch offices are maintained in Syracuse, N.Y., Rutland, Vt., and Park Forest, Ill.

From 1923 until 1963, the late R. C. Carrick, secretary-treasurer, served as NGM's executive officer. The present management includes J. C. Farmer, chairman of the board; K. P. Colby, president; H. H. Metzger, treasurer; and H. R. Lindberg, secretary and general counsel.

Grange Insurance Association, Seattle, Wash.

Organized on April 19, 1894, as the Washington Fire Relief Association, Grange Insurance Association was then to operate strictly within the state of Washington as a fraternal fire association. In June, 1936, the name of the company was changed to its present name and its charter has subsequently been amended to include Idaho, Oregon, Montana, Wyoming, Colorado, and California with the endorsement of each State Grange.

Grange Insurance Association has had a distinguished history of service to Grange members in its area. It has grown to where it now writes a full line of modern farm and casualty coverages, with a premium income in 1965 of $7.8 million and assets of over $10¼ million. Service is confined strictly to members of the Grange, and the Association works closely with the State Granges in the states in which it operates. It is organized and operated as a farmer cooperative, paying back to the insured members in the form of a revolving patronage dividend, the difference between premiums paid and losses sustained. These refunds since 1938 through 1965 total $10.4 million.

The Association owns and occupies a modern three-story office building in Seattle, and seven regional offices modernly equipped, all staffed with 250 employees.

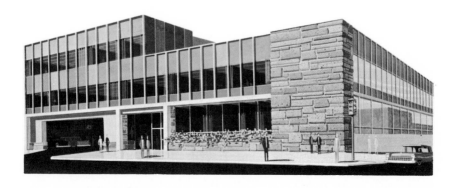

NEW HOME of Grange Insurance Association, Seattle, Wash.

ARCHITECT'S drawing of how Grange Mutual Life Company, headquarters in Nampa, Idaho, will look when completed.

Grange Mutual Life Company, Nampa, Idaho

Grange Mutual Life Company was created for Grange people because of the economic need which developed in the mid-thirties. W. W. Deal, then Master of the Idaho State Grange and later Chaplain of the National Grange, with the help of loyal Grange leaders and members in both Idaho and Washington, chartered this new life company to write life insurance for Grange members on a legal reserve basis.

Since that time, Grange Mutual Life has grown to a healthy $12 million in admitted assets, with $71 million of life insurance in force, and approximately $1 million in policyholders surplus. This Grange company operates in nine states: Washington, Oregon, Montana, Idaho, California, Colorado, Wyoming, Iowa, and Nebraska, and offers a full line of modern life, accident, and health insurance programs.

The Board of Directors of Grange Mutual Life is composed of nine prominent Grange members of long standing. The Grange is a dominant part of GML, and this Grange company continues to cooperate closely with the State Granges in those states in which it is licensed to do business as well as with the National Grange.

A brand new home office building was dedicated in 1961, presumed to be adequate for at least 10 to 15 years. The results of the five-year expansion program inaugurated in 1963, however, made it necessary to increase the home office space and facilities and a construction program is currently under way which will approximately double the floor space of this home office operation.

HEADQUARTERS of Patrons Mutual
Insurance Company, Glastonbury, Conn.

Patrons Mutual Insurance Company of Connecticut, Glastonbury, Conn.

This company has been providing insurance protection for Grange members only since its organization in 1887. Originally their writings were confined to Connecticut. The service and savings have been extended to Massachusetts, Florida, and West Virginia Grange members.

They enjoy an A-plus rating in Best *Insurance Guide*—the highest rating obtainable. Patrons Mutual has a comprehensive program to aid the Granges in its territory.

A communication medium is its *Patrons Plugger*, a publication going into each Subordinate Grange and to the official Grange family in the four-state area. The recent innovation of a *Farmowners Policy*, the first in New England, is designed to give the Grange farm family a package policy of protection.

Their growth throughout the years has been consistent; the result of loyal directors, personnel, agents, and all members of the Grange organization.

National Federation of Grange Mutual Insurance Companies

Organized in November, 1934, and incorporated by a special Act of the Connecticut Legislature effective July 1, 1947, this National Federation provides a clearing house for the reinsurance of risks insured by member companies.

Such member companies may be any Mutual Insurance Company which (a) confines its business to Grange members, or (b) which has been designated by the National Grange, or any State Grange as an official Grange insurance company.

Only such companies may be members of this National Federation which was set up to engage in activities to benefit and protect all member Grange insurance companies.

Twenty member companies which write fire, life, and casualty insurance now belong to the Federation.

ENGLAND'S PRIME MINISTER WELCOMES IFAP DELEGATES—*National Master Herschel D. Newsom introduces Prime Minister Sir Harold Wilson to delegates of the International Federation of Agricultural Producers in London. The Prime Minister spoke at the opening of the 15th IFAP general conference in Agriculture House, in May, 1966.*

The two-week meeting for agricultural leaders from 22 countries marked IFAP'S 20th anniversary.

(L to r) E. W. McCallum, Pres., Federated Farmers of New Zealand, incoming IFAP President; Fred Peart, Minister of Agriculture, Fisheries and Food, United Kingdom; Prime Minister Wilson; and Grange Master Newsom, President of IFAP.

(At right) Bill Williams, President National Farmers Union of England, Scotland, and Northern Ireland; and Roger Savary, Secretary General, IFAP.

17

What the Grange Stands for in

International Affairs

As the Grange grew in influence in the United States, and as farmers throughout the world heard about the success of its program for helping America's farm population, it was inevitable for Grange leaders to be called upon for counsel and recommendations as to international impacts that affected Grange members, and all U.S. farmers, as well as farmers throughout the world.

PRESIDENT JOHNSON addressing the first Session of the Advisory Committee on Trade Negotiations, April 21,1964. A long-time Grange member and the President's Special Representative for Trade Negotiations may be seen at President Johnson's immediate left—the Honorable Christian A. Herter, former Governor of Massachusetts; and former United States Secretary of State. The National Master at extreme right has served as a member of this Public Advisory Committee since its creation.

Since the early 1900's and its 50th anniversary, the Grange has increasingly been active in world affairs to the point where its leaders are an important influence in today's tremendous effort to spread the best agricultural know-how to developing countries, and to utilize every possible means to reduce the starvation doom that increasingly faces millions of people.

It has been said that half the people of the world daily go to bed hungry. For many years, the Grange's great purpose has been to support and work energetically for programs that will provide an adequate diet for more and more people.

Appearing in March, 1966 before a Congressional Committee in support of the *Food For Freedom* legislation, the Master of the National Grange, speaking also as President of the International Federation of Agricultural Producers, and Chairman of the Committee on the World Food Crisis, made this keynote statement:

> The Grange and IFAP have clear, established records of concern for the development of programs to meet human needs, for expanding international trade on a sound basis and for agricultural development—both in developed and developing nations. . . .

We live today in a world of strange and baffling paradoxes. We know more about how to produce and prepare high-quality food for maximum nutritional value than at any time in history; yet we have the bleak prospect that many people will starve to death this year, and the prospects for adequate diet for the rapidly expanding population will become increasingly dim.

In our Western Civilization, we have developed the highest and best techniques of distribution of food products in all of history. Yet, a substantial part of the world is hungry simply because there exists no marketing and transportation organization adequate to move foodstuffs into the food-deficit areas.

We know more about nutrition for both humans and animals than ever before, yet two-thirds of the world suffers from malnutrition, and in some parts of the world, over half the children born die before they reach school age because of inadequate and improper diet. . . .

Due to the technological advancement in the agricultural production of the U.S., the British Commonwealth countries, Western Europe, and parts of South America, we are now able to produce food far beyond the ability of any normal market arrangement to absorb and distribute. Therefore, while the world suffers from a lack of available productive land in the food-deficit areas, the United States has some 50 million acres of land reserves. The developed world and some of the developing countries, including those in grave danger of mass starvation, are spending billions of dollars for military purposes. But they cannot afford the capital necessary to provide food and fiber for a needy world. . . .

In short, we know how to feed the world, and we probably have enough resources in the world, if properly harnessed, to provide an adequate diet for the present and projected population, but we have not found an effective way to provide the food necessary from our American productive capacity to prevent starvation and upgrade diets and to insist that the rest of the developed countries of the world share the burden with us.

How the Grange Became a World Agricultural Leader

Today's established international position of the Grange, and the recognition the organization and its leaders have earned, all came about because of the initiative, straight-thinking, and practical approaches that have characterized Grange involvement in world affairs. The way the Grange develops its policies and builds the backing of its thousands of

COOPERATING IN-TERNATIONALLY — German youth exchangee Winfrid Hollerbach confers with a National Grange youth representative. The National Grange has sponsored visits to the U. S. for over 900 youths from countries abroad in the last 16 years.

members for national and international governmental projects is basic and unique. Over 600 meetings are held each weekday night of thousands of thoughtful, down-to-earth Grange members. The Patrons who participate are people who, by their very nature and by reason of the fraternal, ritualistic structure of the organization which brings them together, are characterized by their respect for each other and for other people. They base their conclusions on respect for property rights, as well as individual, personal rights of the other person. This characteristic arises in part from the fact that they live in open country, in God's out-of-doors; but also it arises in part out of the fraternal climate that dominates Grange meetings, where there is a ritualistic ceremony that cultivates the mind, and puts it into proper order to think straight, reasonably, and equitably.

Their discussions of national and world problems and the best ways to deal with them, give support and confidence to state and national Grange leaders in their dealings with high governmental officials and with international organizations of farmers.

An enthusiastic Grange member's idea started it all. Grange Historian Charles M. Gardner tells the story of David Lubin, an enthusiastic California Patron, who conceived the idea of an International Institute of Agriculture. It was his dream that a permanent agency be set up in which nations throughout the world would be represented, and which would have established headquarters, be financed internationally, and devote its energies largely to research work along practical lines of world agriculture. King Victor Emmanuel III of Italy became very interested in this project and in 1905 the proposed agency was set up in permanent quarters at Rome, eventually becoming an international spokesman for agriculture with more than 60 different nations represented.

This first attempt at international collaboration united the nations in a program for improved farm conditions and started the effort for greater unity among agricultural groups and peoples. Far-reaching results came from this start, such as the Food and Agriculture Organization of the United Nations, and the International Federation of Agricultural Producers.

From the very beginning the Grange was involved in all of these developments. For example, President Coolidge in 1926 named National Master Louis J. Taber as one of the delegates to the International Institute of Agriculture. His close personal inspection of agricultural conditions in Denmark and adjacent countries was the forerunner of similar contributions by his successors, National Masters Albert S. Goss and Herschel D. Newsom, who brought back to Grange sessions and to their National Capital contacts, a wealth of information and a broader understanding of world agricultural problems.

IFAP Founded

It was during the administration of National Master Goss that the greatest advances were made in world agricultural organization, both among governments and among farmers' own organizations. Following a conference of nations at Hot Springs, Va. to consider the problems of food and agriculture called by President Roosevelt, a second meeting in Quebec in 1945 included National Master Goss, as an Advisor. Through his efforts due recognition was given the work for 40 years of the International Institute of Agriculture which was consolidated with the new FAO (Food and Agriculture Organization).

Soon thereafter independent non-governmental farm organizations from seven nations met in Quebec to consider the creation of an independent federation of farm organizations to bring the farmers of the world together to meet world food problems, and to protect the interests of producers.

Mr. Goss was very active in this and in the meeting in May, 1946, in London, at which representatives from 31 nations formed the International Federation of Agricultural Producers (IFAP). Mr. Goss represented the Grange at international food conferences and had much to contribute to the policies adopted, and in helping to build the IFAP into a strong organization.

Grange contributions to the IFAP and all that it means to American farmers to be a vital part of world agriculture were emphasized by the three years as President of the IFAP that National Master Herschel D. Newsom has just completed.

Importance of Farmer Organization Stressed

In Church House, London, England, on May 3, 1966 in his 20th anniversary address as IFAP President, National Master Newsom, speaking from the rich background of the Granges' 100 years of leadership in American agriculture, made this significant statement about organized farmers. He was paralleling developments in the U.S. in which the Grange has had such prominent part, with comparable developments in other leading countries of the world. He said:

> Twenty years ago—as today—farm leaders believed that farming could only be prosperous when farmers joined together to understand and tackle their problems of production and marketing. Twenty years ago—as today—farm leaders realized that an ever-improving productivity was the master key to progress. And this is the place to remind those who might tend to overlook it, that few—if any— countries have seen the improvement in agricultural productivity matched by comparable performance by the other sectors of the economy. Nor have there been any more illustrations of general economic advance without agricultural progress having preceded such industrial or economic development.

NATIONAL MASTER Herschel D. Newsom and other members of the Public Advisory Board on Foreign Operations. (Advisory to the President of the United States.) They are taking the Oath of Office in 1953.

Twenty years ago—as today—farm leaders agreed that a trusting partnership between farmers' organizations and governments is essential if constructive farm policies are to be implemented. Twenty years ago—as today—farm leaders recognized agriculture's responsibility to consumers.

As we went along we came to realize how deep was the community of interest between primary producers the world over and how fruitful were our continuing consultations amongst farmers' representatives . . .

In rich and poor countries alike, primary producers have to denounce the symmetrical illusions of laissez faire—which creates chaos and favors exploitation of the weak by the strong—and of complete state control—which stifles individual initiative and breeds inefficiency. In rich and poor countries alike, primary producers have to limit or regulate speculation—of which the prime victims are always those at the base of the economic structure, that is to say, the farmers themselves. We as farmers in our respective countries, therefore, must promote formulae of economic and trade organization which create a basis for the stability necessary to harmonious progress.

It is natural that, with the interest of the Grange in feeding the hungry people of the world, it should become active in many segments of this great problem with tremendous implications involving peace and war, the freeing up of trade restrictions between nations, prevention of economic disruption of domestic markets, sale of surplus farm commodities to communist nations, and various positions on tariffs. How the Grange stands on these matters and the multitude of details involved in international affairs are constantly reviewed through the unique machinery of the Grange, which encourages members everywhere to "have their say on what Grange policies should be."

THE GRANGE COOPERATES AT ALL LEVELS—Close contact is maintained by Grange officials and the U. S. Department of Agriculture. Here U.S.D.A. Secretary Orville Freeman and National Master Herschel D. Newsom discuss plans to upgrade rural life.

18

What the Grange Stands for in

National Welfare

Not Selfishly for Rural Progress Only

From the date of organization of the Grange itself, as well as throughout the recorded discussions of the Founders, it became clear that the Founders wanted—and indeed succeeded in setting up—an organizational structure that would encourage and induce the members to become well-rounded, knowledgeable, and active citizens of their own community and their country as a whole.

Though the basic structure of the Grange was, and will ever be, an agricultural structure, and though its beautiful agricultural ritualism preaches eloquently of the dignity of labor and of the beauty of rural life, Grange Founders did not even, in the beginning of the organization's history, confine their planning to farm and agricultural matters alone.

Being men of broad vision and of great ability, they succeeded in building an organizational structure predicated on the steadfastness, basic patriotism, and the solid worth of the farm and rural population. Their plan was designed to exploit the personal qualities of these people to help build a great country, even amidst the chaos which then existed in many rural areas following the Great War Between the States.

They took the first steps *to position* the Grange not only as an organization dealing with problems of the farm and rural life, but also dealing with many other matters affecting the total national welfare.

CONFERRING WITH PRESIDENT EISENHOWER ON GRANGE RECOM-
MENDATIONS—National Grange Executive Committee, officers, and staff members
meet with President Dwight D. Eisenhower and True D. Morse, Under Secretary
of Agriculture.

A very early important venture, which developed naturally out of the
farmers' concern with transportation of their produce and needed supplies,
rates and services of the railroads, was their successful fight leading to
enactment of the Granger Laws and the first state and national control of
all public utilities. (See Chapter 6, "The Granger Laws—Their Significance.")

No Infringement on Individual Freedom, Opportunity

Over the years since its very beginning the Grange has interested itself
in all matters that involved *any infringement upon maximum individual
freedom and opportunity*—not alone for the few, but for all people.

A Grange explanatory statement says it well:

> National welfare depends upon decisions we make and upon the collective and
> individual action we take as free people in a democratic society.

> We seek for ourselves, and for generations to follow, the preservation and en-
> hancement of a heritage providing maximum individual freedom consistent with
> "the greatest good for the greatest number," economically, socially and spiritually.

> For a number of years there has been a gradual trend toward centralization of
> Government authority and responsibility. This trend is a matter of deep concern
> to the Grange—and to all people who believe in our Constitutional form of gov-
> ernment in which all power rests, ultimately, with the people.

Basic Grange Position on General Situations

Here are examples of how the Grange speaks out on broad matters of national welfare:

POWER OF GOVERNMENT

Grange policy reaffirms support for the freedom of state and local governments from encroachment by Federal Government. It insists that powers not specifically delegated to Federal Government by the U.S. Constitution (or prohibited by it to states) are reserved for the states or people. It also recognizes the separate functions of the legislative, administrative, and judiciary branches of Government and is opposed to the encroachment of either upon the functions of another.

LABOR RELATIONS

The Grange recognizes the complementary interests of agriculture and labor; it will support this community of interest to the fullest extent possible under constructive policy.

The Grange is opposed to monopoly control—whether exercised by an individual, a corporation, a labor union or any other organization. Thus, provisions of laws to prevent the abuse of monopolistic powers of corporations should apply to labor unions as well.

PROOF IN LENDING

There is need for legislation requiring all finance and insurance charges to be clearly itemized with the total specifically reported to the borrower, or recipient of services, in terms of "a simple annual rate" on the unpaid balance of the obligation.

TEACHERS

The Grange will continue to support programs to provide adequate incentives to attract and hold competent teachers. It advocates that development and acceptance of programs and practices to reward teachers according to ability and performance, and in return, urges teachers to avoid action which tends to reduce public respect for their profession.

SCHOOL FINANCING

The Grange favors equalization of the school support tax burden and believes that dependence upon a single tax source is unwise; property taxes for school purposes should be supplemented by revenue from other sources.

GOVERNMENT IN BUSINESS

Government should withdraw from businesses which can feasibly be operated by private enterprise. The U.S. Employment Service should confine its activities to providing employment services which are voluntarily requested by employees and employers and should not enter the field of regulation.

DOUBLE TAXATION

Because the Grange is opposed to double taxation in any form, it will oppose elimination of state gasoline taxes, vehicle fees and similar taxes already paid, as allowable deduction for Federal income tax purposes. Proposals to reduce or disallow deduction for property taxes and interest are also opposed.

VOCATIONAL EDUCATION

The continuing need for secondary vocational agricultural training, in support of our traditional family farm pattern of agriculture, is recognized and the Grange supports measures to strengthen the vocational agricultural curricula to discourage high school dropouts, as well as technical training for non-farm occupations.

CLEAR CHANNEL BROADCASTING

Currently and potentially, adequately powered "clear channel" radio stations offer the only feasible means of providing satisfactory night-time radio service to millions of rural Americans living in well over 50 percent of the nation's land area. The Grange will vigorously oppose any further duplication of frequencies now assigned to clear channel stations. It would further urge authorization of clear channel station use of additional power necessary to provide adequate night-time radio service to the millions of Americans living in rural areas and not now receiving such service.

TELEVISION CHANNELS

Support for the adoption and implementation of a television channel allocation policy which will assure that existing television service to rural areas will be maintained and improved, is reaffirmed. Any proposals which would result in action impairing or destroying existing television service to rural areas will be opposed by the Grange.

EMINENT DOMAIN

The Grange reaffirms its stand in opposition to the extension of the power of Eminent Domain in any form which does not fully safeguard the interests of the owner. Each party should be entitled to an appraiser, and in addition, a third impartial appraiser should be provided. We oppose the condemnation of agricultural land for recreational or military use when other land is available.

RESOURCE DEVELOPMENT AND USE

The water and land policy of the U.S. is haphazard, erratic and often contradictory. The Grange feels that the Nation can no longer delay a serious study of the conservation and the utilization of natural resources, especially in regard to water and land. Such a study should concern itself with projected needs for water and land, the sources from which these needs are to be supplied, and the means that are to be used to insure the public the benefits of such a program.

The Grange seeks national resource policies and programs which will, while protecting the rights and interests of individuals most directly involved, give major emphasis to local, state, regional, and national needs, in that order.

The foregoing are but a few of the many current policy positions of the Grange on matters of concern to all citizens. Annually, Grange Headquarters publishes a booklet entitled, "Summary of Legislative Policies & Programs." The 1966 booklet had 52 pages.

Wave of Tomorrow

The National Grange has received much praise for its Young Married's program, introduced in 1961 to give recognition to young married people and give them more opportunity through the Grange for fellowship with other young couples, for association with others having similar interests, for community recognition and leadership.

One of the key features of the program is the selection of the "Young Couple of the Year." Everett and Irma Holstein of Blair, Nebr., were the 1965 National Winners, being honored for their outstanding accomplishments at the Topeka, Kans., Annual Meeting.

The Grange Tomorrow

To worthy families—rural and urban—The Grange extends an invitation to participate at a time when there is ever-increasing need for a rededication and united support of the principles of individual integrity and fair dealing among men at home and throughout the world.

The Grange offers the opportunity to worthy individuals to use their abilities as part of a united effort to expand freedom at home and abroad, to speed progress, and to enlarge the horizon of the American family for service and abundant living.

—HERSCHEL D. NEWSOM

Pattern for the
Second Century

In the foregoing pages there has been briefed—often too much condensed—the dramatic story of the soul-satisfying, enjoyable, personal growth, and service-to-others features of Grange membership and the almost-beyond-belief local, state, and national services that the Grange has performed for nearly 100 years to improve communities, states, and the national well-being; and to influence our government as a servant of all Americans.

The question is paramount now as to whether this "First Century of Service and Evolution" should, without modification, become the foundation for the Grange's second century.

While it is clear that much of the character, development, and achievement of this second century is already cast, members of the Grange during this Centennial Year need to think deeply, discuss at length, and act courageously to extend the effectiveness of all Grange principles and activities.

Not only must the Grange keep on doing better the splendid things it has been doing, but members and leaders must seek to recognize and reclaim lost opportunities to improve the effectiveness of all Grange units as community builders.

Here, gleaned from recent statements of a few of the many Grange leaders who have thought deeply about the future of the Grange, are quotes which should be pondered—not alone by Grange members— but also by all who live in this great country which the Grange influenced in the past—and which this same Grange will doubtless be seeking to direct or influence in the future to the very limit of its ability to do so! Space does not permit use of all, and the selection by the author has been cruelly restricted by space limitations.

Five Features of the Grange of Tomorrow

1. The community center for an area—the one spot where people of a common concern and interest, from nearby homes can come together as a group.

2. The Grange will have to be a recreational center in a much bigger sense than it is, depending upon its "community."

3. The Grange will be known for its public forum—a debating place on any or all issues; a legislative action center with candidates really seeking an invitation to be interviewed; a center where major local problems will be solved by local people in a democratic way.

4. The Grange will be the "service eye" of the area. Those truly down on their luck will be stimulated and assisted back to self-sufficiency; the forgotten will be remembered; the handicapped will be assisted to places of self-support.

5. The Grange will lead a crusade to appreciate U.S.A., to keep it free, to improve our image abroad.

Increased Devotion Needed

The Grange has served the family farm, but linked the villages and the ruralists into an urban life. Through its family memberships of adolescent youth and parents, it helped to bring about a family stability which developed individuals to higher potentialities by rubbing elbows with their peers in discussion, in debate, in committees. Taking the message of the Grange to legislative bodies, local, state, and national, it promoted the community and today, hundreds of our new cities in America owe their creation and support to the Grangers out in the hills where the creek forks.

The Grange tomorrow will continue this history of the past. Grange leaders and patrons will learn to adapt its formula of community service to the changing end of the 20th and the beginning of the 21st Centuries. Its voice is needed, as it has been for a century, in the legislative halls and business assemblies.

In order to fulfill its date with destiny, the Grange must have increasing devotion from its members—new and old, young and adult—in helping to put ideas into words and to receive ideas from others and to transmit them back at the Grange halls in thousands of communities. Information travels best on a two-way street, and the Grange must continue to give and to receive information in the public interest.

To Raise the Level of Human Existence

On the National Scene, with headquarters in the nerve center of the mightiest nation in history, the Grange will advance new ideas for national growth. It can represent workable plans for world-wide activity that will raise the level of human existence in every corner of the globe.

Developing Leadership and Understanding

Perhaps never before has the need for a vigorous Grange effort, and of broad American community understanding, and effort to develop leadership, been so great.

It is essential that we accept our proportionate responsibility to help develop a sound and intelligent concept of the proper and appropriate role and function of our agricultural and rural life, in the minds of our fellow Americans.

Perpetuation of Mutual Concern, Fraternal Friendship

The greatest challenge to "The Grange of Tomorrow" will be the preservation and perpetuation of "Mutual Concern" and "Fraternal Fellowship" in a world that expects to buy everything (including their soul's salvation) with cold cash.

"The Grange of Tomorrow" through its Fraternal, Family, Social, Educational, and Legislative structure will prove that "The best things in life are free"; that our motto, "In essentials unity, in non-essentials Liberty and in all things Charity" is the very essence of self-government with a maximum of individual freedom.

Be Ready for Youth

The "avalanche" of young adults is exploding into our midst! The Grange can be ready for them and should be ready to accept them into membership. The Grange must be prepared to offer them a "choice." Some will choose the Grange. Others will not. Those who do choose the Grange will do so only if the Grange is a vehicle which demonstrates its ability to serve in modern times, which demonstrates its readiness for the questions, the curiosity, and the restlessness of young people.

Continue Work Upon the Immortal Mind

The Grange tomorrow will be the instrument which will bring understanding and close association between the rural and urban people as together they teach the Grange ritualism. Old as it is, it still teaches us that there is a Supreme Being who provides a seed time and a harvest time and that the most important thing to work upon is the immortal mind. As our ritual states, "If we work upon marble it will crumble; if we work upon brass time will corrode it; if we rear temples, they will crumble into dust; but if we work upon the immortal mind, imbue them with just and true principles, the reverence of God and the love of our fellowman we engrave upon something that will brighten unto all eternity." This we are doing in the Grange and will continue to do in the tomorrows that are before us.

Venture into New Fields

With more young people leaving the farm and the farm population diminishing, the Grange must accept the challenge to meet the needs of all its members. In our second century we will venture into new fields. One of these will be new ideas in education. As more and more Granges find themselves within urban areas in our second century, we will need to develop a greater understanding between the rural and urban people.

A Forum for Leadership Training

The Grange can be a forum in every Grange community from which real down-to-earth-grass-roots-leadership is trained and the individual developed. Some of the great rural leaders of the past century have been *Grange-trained* men and women! This has been especially true in recent years in the Home Economics work of the Grange over the nation. This development of the individual in the Grange is evidenced by the fact that these Grange-trained individuals are so often chosen as leaders by other groups.

Every person who has a rural mail box or receives a parcel by mail is indebted to the Grange. These came as the result of *organized* effort. The appeal of the single individual has some effect, nationally. The appeal of a large, respected, and recognized group multiplies this effect many, many times. This will be truer than ever during the years ahead. The Grange furnishes a powerful "line of communication" direct from the community "back home" to the national capital.

Appendix

ANNUAL SESSIONS OF THE NATIONAL GRANGE

Session No.	Year	Place	Master	Seventh Degree Initiates
	1867, Dec. 4	Washington, D. C.	Birthday	
1	1868, Jan.	Washington, D. C.	Wm. Saunders	
2	1869, Apr.	Washington, D. C.	Wm. Saunders	
3	1870, Jan.	Washington, D. C.	Wm. Saunders	
4	1871, Jan.	Washington, D. C.	Wm. Saunders	
5	1872, Jan.	Washington, D. C.	Wm. Saunders	
6	1873, Jan.	Georgetown, D. C.	Wm. Saunders	
7	1874, Feb.	St. Louis, Mo.	D. W. Adams	
8	1875, Feb.	Charleston, S. C.	D. W. Adams	
9	1875, Nov.	Louisville, Ky.	D. W. Adams	
10	1876, Nov.	Chicago, Illinois	John T. Jones	
11	1877, Nov.	Cincinnati, Ohio	John T. Jones	
12	1878, Nov.	Richmond, Va.	S. E. Adams	
13	1879, Nov.	Canandaigua, N. Y.	S. E. Adams	
14	1880, Nov.	Washington, D. C.	J. J. Woodman	
15	1881, Nov.	Washington, D. C.	J. J. Woodman	
16	1882, Nov.	Indianapolis, Ind.	J. J. Woodman	
17	1883, Nov.	Washington, D. C.	J. J. Woodman	
18	1884, Nov.	Nashville, Tenn.	J. J. Woodman	8
19	1885, Nov.	Boston, Mass.	J. J. Woodman	19
20	1886, Nov.	Philadelphia, Pa.	Put Darden	33
21	1887, Nov.	Lansing, Mich.	Put Darden	17
22	1888, Nov.	Topeka, Kan.	James Draper	83
23	1889, Nov.	Sacramento, Calif.	J. H. Brigham	340
24	1890, Nov.	Atlanta, Ga.	J. H. Brigham	27
25	1891, Nov.	Springfield, Ohio	J. H. Brigham	429
26	1892, Nov.	Concord, N. H.	J. H. Brigham	1,342
27	1893, Nov.	Syracuse, N. Y.	J. H. Brigham	275
28	1894, Nov.	Springfield, Ill.	J. H. Brigham	226
29	1895, Nov.	Worcester, Mass.	J. H. Brigham	1,318
30	1896, Nov.	Washington, D. C.	J. H. Brigham	83
31	1897, Nov.	Harrisburg, Pa.	J. H. Brigham	313
32	1898, Nov.	Concord, N. H.	Aaron Jones	1,047
33	1899, Nov.	Springfield, Ohio	Aaron Jones	443
34	1900, Nov.	Washington, D. C.	Aaron Jones	116
35	1901, Nov.	Lewiston, Me.	Aaron Jones	1,750
36	1902, Nov.	Lansing, Mich.	Aaron Jones	600
37	1903, Nov.	Rochester, N. Y.	Aaron Jones	620
38	1904, Nov.	Portland, Ore.	Aaron Jones	963
39	1905, Nov.	Atlantic City, N. J.	Aaron Jones	1,117
40	1906, Nov.	Denver, Colo.	N. J. Bachelder	125
41	1907, Nov.	Hartford, Conn.	N. J. Bachelder	2,490
42	1908, Nov.	Washington, D. C.	N. J. Bachelder	458
43	1909, Nov.	Des Moines, Iowa	N. J. Bachelder	60
44	1910, Nov.	Atlantic City, N. J.	N. J. Bachelder	683
45	1911, Nov.	Columbus, Ohio	N. J. Bachelder	786
46	1912, Nov.	Spokane, Wash.	Oliver Wilson	201
47	1913, Nov.	Manchester, N. H.	Oliver Wilson	5,459
48	1914, Nov.	Wilmington. Del.	Oliver Wilson	768
49	1915, Nov.	Oakland, Calif.	Oliver Wilson	326
50	1916, Nov.	Washington, D. C.	Oliver Wilson	723
51	1917, Nov.	St. Louis, Mo.	Oliver Wilson	147
52	1918, Nov.	Syracuse, N. Y.	Oliver Wilson	1,524
53	1919, Nov.	Grand Rapids, Mich.	Oliver Wilson	1,614

ANNUAL SESSIONS OF THE NATIONAL GRANGE (Continued)

Session No.	Year	Place	Master	Seventh Degree Initiates
54	1920, Nov.	Boston, Mass.	S. J. Lowell	9,838
55	1921, Nov.	Portland, Ore.	S. J. Lowell	1,200
56	1922, Nov.	Wichita, Kans.	S. J. Lowell	629
57	1923, Nov.	Pittsburgh, Pa.	S. J. Lowell	3,993
58	1924, Nov.	Atlantic City, N. J.	L. J. Taber	2,032
59	1925, Nov.	Sacramento, Calif.	L. J. Taber	816
60	1926, Nov.	Portland, Me.	L. J. Taber	7,236
61	1927, Nov.	Cleveland, Ohio	L. J. Taber	5,811
62	1928, Nov.	Washington, D. C.	L. J. Taber	2,708
63	1929, Nov.	Seattle, Wash.	L. J. Taber	1,997
64	1930, Nov.	Rochester, N. Y.	L. J. Taber	11,125
65	1931, Nov.	Madison, Wis.	L. J. Taber	721
66	1932, Nov.	Winston-Salem, N. C.	L. J. Taber	1,665
67	1933, Nov.	Boise, Idaho	L. J. Taber	951
68	1934, Nov.	Hartford, Conn.	L. J. Taber	12,679
69	1935, Nov.	Sacramento, Calif.	L. J. Taber	1,652
70	1936, Nov.	Columbus, Ohio	L. J. Taber	7,218
71	1937, Nov.	Harrisburg, Pa.	L. J. Taber	6,715
72	1938, Nov.	Portland, Ore.	L. J. Taber	3,781
73	1939, Nov.	Peoria, Ill.	L. J. Taber	1,147
74	1940, Nov.	Syracuse, N. Y.	L. J. Taber	5,256
75	1941, Nov.	Worcester, Mass.	L. J. Taber	12,999
76	1942, Nov.	Wenatchee, Wash.	A. S. Goss	1,715
77	1943, Nov.	Grand Rapids, Mich.	A. S. Goss	2,022
78	1944, Nov.	Winston-Salem, N. C.	A. S. Goss	1,295
79	1945, Nov.	Kansas City, Mo.	A. S. Goss	1,611
80	1946, Nov.	Portland, Ore.	A. S. Goss	5,766
81	1947, Nov.	Columbus, Ohio	A. S. Goss	18,374
82	1948, Nov.	Portland, Me.	A. S. Goss	17,277
83	1949, Nov.	Sacramento, Calif.	A. S. Goss	4,001
84	1950, Nov.	Minneapolis, Minn.	Henry D. Sherwood	1,266
85	1951, Nov.	Atlantic City, N. J.	Herschel D. Newsom	9,233
86	1952, Nov.	Rockford, Ill.	Herschel D. Newsom	2,373
87	1953, Nov.	Burlington, Vt.	Herschel D. Newsom	7,140
88	1954, Nov.	Spokane, Wash.	Herschel D. Newsom	5,040
89	1955, Nov.	Cleveland, Ohio	Herschel D. Newsom	7,179
90	1956, Nov.	Rochester, N. Y.	Herschel D. Newsom	5,547
91	1957, Nov.	Colorado Spring, Col.	Herschel D. Newsom	1,193
92	1958, Nov.	Grand Rapids, Mich.	Herschel D. Newsom	1,309
93	1959, Nov.	Long Beach, Calif.	Herschel D. Newsom	1,979
94	1960, Nov.	Winston-Salem, N. C.	Herschel D. Newsom	1,549
95	1961, Nov.	Worcester, Mass.	Herschel D. Newsom	8,229
96	1962, Nov.	Fort Wayne, Ind.	Herschel D. Newsom	2,391
97	1963, Nov.	Portland, Ore.	Herschel D. Newsom	5,445
98	1964, Nov.	Atlantic City, N. J.	Herschel D. Newsom	3,678
99	1965, Nov.	Topeka, Kan.	Herschel D. Newsom	1,023
100	1966, Nov.	Minneapolis, Minn.		
101	1967, Nov.	Syracuse, N. Y.		
102	1968, Nov.	Peoria, Ill.		
103	1969	Florida*		
104	1970	Idaho*		

*Host state selected by Delegate Body five years in advance. Host city has not yet been determined by Executive Committee.

Index